See Salt Tears

By Blanche Haddow

Copyright © 2025 Blanche Haddow
All rights reserved.
ISBN: 9798287604738

Please Note

This book is about a journey through health and so uses some words about bodily functions etc. Not words that I, myself, would particularly, usually want to read, but they are part of the story and so they are being left in.

There are many times in this book where my head is all a muddle. That is also part of the journey and the story and so, where I could, I have left these bits in.

The journey moves through many thoughts, feelings and muddles both good and bad. My views and ideas are purely that, and not in any way advising anyone else. It is your life and completely up to you what you do with it. I would, personally, advise to love and respect yourself and then, in turn, you will be able to love and respect everything and everyone.

I would also advise, always seeking professional advice for any ailments, worries, health issues etc. These professionals are trained and experienced, they are there to help.

As for any unusual lumps. Well, I would again, advise going to see about it. Either there is nothing to worry about, so you can put your mind at rest, or there is, in which case the quicker you go and get it dealt with, the better.

Disclaimer

All pictures and contents of this book belong to and are created by Blanche Haddow (unless otherwise stated).

The contents of this book are purely my own thoughts and feelings (current at time of writing).

Always seek professional advice for any health conditions etc.

Dedication

There are so many people that have been here for me throughout this journey, friends, family, NHS (National Health Service) staff, and others.

Many whom I want to thank, so much, for all their help, patience, support, love etc. But you will find out who they are by reading this book.

So, apart from that, I am going to dedicate this book to the incredible, amazing, brilliant, caring, fun, cheery, calm, extremely hardworking, professional staff at the:

Oncology Day Patient Unit
(Perth Royal Infirmary)

You are all angels, and I want to say thank you so much for all and everything that you do in your incredible work.

"You don't need a magic book as a book is magic!"
Blanche 2024

Contents

The Lump 1
Telling People 8
The Big Scan 19
The Start of It All 24
September 2023 27
October 2023 49
November 2023 65
December 2023 82
January 2024 88
February 2024 108
March 2024 153
April 2024 169
May 2024 189
June and July 2024 204
September 2024 211
October and November 2024 217
Newton's Cradle 223
References 226
Meet the Author 228

The Lump

The lump that I thought might be there, really was, not something that I wanted to know nor think about.

Luckily, being a lady of over 50 years of age I happened to get a letter inviting me for the routine mammogram test that they offer to us, periodically, over a period spanning 20 years. That is not a letter, invitation or thing that I ever usually want to receive.

Double luckily, we now get to visit a mobile unit for our routine mammograms in our own town. So, when it was time for the appointment, off I went. Just down the road from where I live.

There were no troubles. The two ladies, staff, were lovely. I sort of get led around in a dwam (Scottish word for not really knowing what is going on or dream like state) as they give us instructions, get changed, take off this, put on that, stand there, hold your arms this way, stand that way. A few questions. Some uncomfortable machine squeezing and that is it, over and done with, for another few years.

It is a bit awkward as you see other ladies that you recognise as they are around the same age as you and this is a small town, but then we are all going through the same, not particularly wanted, examination. I must say that it is a million times better than the blooming smear test though!

The ladies were so lovely, helpful and friendly that when walking past their mobile unit, the next day, I thought about ordering them some flowers to thank them. I never did. But thoughts and best wishes can do good too.

That was in early May, they said it might take about 8 weeks to get the results. By June, I decided that there really was a lump in my right breast or boob as I call it. I did **not** want to know and did **not** want it to be there. But I was very brave and phoned up to make an appointment with the doctor.

I had gone right off making appointments with doctors since the system all changed. It used to be great with my good old family doctor. He knew me well, and my family, and had been my doctor for a long time. He was always running at least ½ an hour late for appointments, but we forgave him because he was so nice. He took time to talk to us.

Now the system has all changed. I don't even know who my doctor is. When I went for one of the Covid vaccinations that we had to have, in Perth (our nearest city) they asked who my doctor was. I didn't know! So, they ended up telling me, but it wasn't a name that I knew or remembered. If I passed my doctor in the street, I would not know who they were. I think that is wrong and sad. However, that was then. I know how lucky we are to have an NHS (National Health Service) and that we shouldn't ever complain and should be extremely grateful. But I still don't like the new system and still don't think that it is the right way to do things.

We now have to phone up for an appointment and then have to tell the person, on the phone, why we want to see the doctor. I am getting more used to this now, they are always lovely, polite and very helpful. But then, I didn't want to do this and certainly didn't want to tell the person on the phone about why I wanted an appointment.

I hardly ever go to the doctors. One of the last times I had phoned up, was just after the Covid lockdown. I had been seeing strange electric lights in front of my eyes and black bits floating down. Once I got through the queue on the phone, the receptionist told me that I had to go and see an optician. That is another thing that I don't like, at all, about the new system. It is so confusing with all the different rules about who you are to go and see about all different symptoms. Before, the doctor just used to talk to you, ask what was wrong and then give you a check, no matter what it was.

So, I was told to get an emergency appointment with an optician. I had only been to the opticians once and it was in Perth. I tried phoning the one in our town, but they said that I had to go to the Perth one as I was registered there. So, I phoned Perth and got an emergency appointment. Luckily, Sue (my step mum) said she would take me through. By this time, I was very worried and stressed about what it might be and why I had been told to go for an emergency appointment. After getting there, and getting lots of tests, I got told that it was a kind of visual migraine. Which was such a relief. I also found it quite ironic, as all that stress would not, I bet, have helped with such a thing!

My previous experience, with the health centre, had been a few years before that. I had a really bad face infection which then got a further infection on top of it. After going to the pharmacist (which they encourage nowadays) I was then advised to go to the doctors and, of course, I had to do that by making a phone call for an appointment. I then got an appointment with a practice nurse. Who said to come back if it got worse. Which it did, much worse, over the weekend. Of course I had to phone up again. I got a phone appointment and had to try and persuade them that it was really bad and was not, I felt, to do with my teeth etc. I ended up off work for a couple of weeks, having to go down to the health centre each day for checks and looking like I had been beaten up.

One very hot summer day, I was on a day out, with my dad, when he said that there was blood on my leg. I looked down and there was a lump, or bite looking thing with blood coming out of it. It turned out, after a day or two, like a big circle mark so I wondered if it might be a tick bite. I went to the pharmacist, and she told me not to wear shorts on my walks! She said that she could not advise me on whether I should check with the doctors, and that it was up to me. Which I found very confusing. So, I ended up phoning, got a phone appointment and sent a photo of the mark. The doctor phoned back and reassured me that it was not a tick bite as it did not have the circle ring pattern. I think I must have just been far too hot, and a vein had burst a bit, or something. Anyway, that also made me feel silly, left me confused about what to do about such things and put me right off going to either the pharmacist or the doctors.

I think that I was talking to the same doctor on the phone. They always ask if there is anything else. I told him that I had been having a very sore lower back. He replied that he was "not unduly worried about that" and that sore backs are very common! So, I felt really silly and decided it was time to stop telling them about that.

But back to now, this lump could not be put off, so, reluctantly, I phoned. They answered quickly, no queue and no problem. I had to tell the receptionist about the lump. I got an appointment for later that same day.

When first writing my notes, for this book, I didn't want to write them, as it would make it real!

I have written in my earlier books, about finding out that I am on the autistic spectrum. Now I have found out that I have breast cancer.

Cancer, like death, is generally not talked about.

It is a really important subject. Writing my thoughts is a thing that I can do well, so I have decided to write this book.

It is Important for people to hear about, know and understand what it can feel like to find out that you have cancer. Also, I believe that it will be very helpful and interesting to hear about it from the viewpoint and perspective of a person on the autistic spectrum. We, people with autism, see, experience and process things in a different way, so books such as these are very important for society to get to know and understand the different way things might be looked at and experienced.

This book is for anyone and everyone. I hope that it helps you to think and understand more about yourself and in turn, others.

I would like to show you, not just what it is or can be like to go through this, my particular journey with this particular type of cancer, but also more of what it is like to experience these things while looking through an autistic lens.

This is a journey that involves health and so I have talked about bodily functions etc. I realise that these are not always pleasant things to read about. I would usually not want to be reading such words myself. However, they are all part of the story and all part of us, that is why I have left them in. So please excuse, and hopefully understand, any use of gunk, farts, sick etc!

(I use simple words for such bodily functions. I am not interested in changing words. It doesn't really make sense to me, to change words. I am not very good with change.

That reminds me of a story from my best friend, Babs, years ago. Her son, Craig, now all grown up, was just a wee boy. Their hamster had died, so they put it, nicely and gently, into a shoe box to take it along to her mums, to be buried in the garden. As they were walking along, Craig said, "I wonder if Snuggles will still pump, when in heaven!")

Right now, I am a bit achy and have a rectangle shaped bruise on the top part of my right boob.

It was a few months ago now, that I went for that mammogram. It was the second routine check-up one that I have had, after having reached the ripe old age of fifty.

I did have one around age 36 which was very scary as that was the same age as my mum had been when she died of cancer, back in the 1970s.

It's funny to have to write 1970s nowadays. I am, just now, finally accepting that the 90s was a long time ago but it is still a very strange thought. My Granny Haddow was actually born in the 1800s!

Back to my 30s, then, very luckily, the lump, that I found in the side of my boob, turned out just to be some small cysts. I was extremely relieved and never told anyone or not many people about it. Even although it seems to be my habit, now, to tell the whole world all about me, by writing books, I am actually a very private person who never really tells people about myself. I don't think people are much interested in hearing other people's stories. But then, we must be, as we love to read or watch about people's lives and experiences. Well, some of us do.

Now more people flick through social media, **not** television. A quick fix. They don't want videos longer than two minutes or that is what we are advised.

So, I knew what to expect when my age won me the reward of a mammogram. I must say that although rather sore, awkward and uncomfortable, there is not much to them. It is a million times better with the machines now without the old heavy metal plates that they had in the machines before. Imagine the fun of having your boobs squashed tight between two metal plates.

Telling People

This book is being written using the notes that I made as I travelled along on my journey. I am going to write them as they are, even if I have changed my mind or thoughts as I have gone along. I feel it is important to illustrate the rollercoaster of a journey that this can be, not just in health but also with thoughts, ideas, feelings etc.

So, I got to see the doctor very quickly. I was on the phone to make an appointment and had to go that same day. The doctor was obviously worried. It is "urgent" as it could spread. She tried but couldn't get the results of the mammogram that I had been for.

The doctor soon phoned me. That was really nice, like the good old doctor days. I have got an appointment for 10th July (2023).

I have told Dad as I will have to ask for a lift and for his company, so I had to tell Sue (my step mum) too. Dad was very upset. It was not nice. Poor Sue got told to go away but then he also wanted a cuddle. It must have been so horrible and confusing for them to hear.

After that, things were fine. We just decided to forget about it, as much as we could, and get on with things. My brother,

Duncan, arrived for a short holiday and my brother, Findlay, and his family, visited on the Sunday. I didn't tell them as I wanted to just enjoy things.

10th July 2023: The day of the appointment in Dundee arrived. It was a lovely day. It went well and we had a nice lunch.

The appointment place was so strange to be in. There were different people waiting to be seen and it was so strange to think that they would all be going through the same thing as me. There were two ladies obviously partners, another lady doing her knitting, a young lady and an old lady.

A few days before the appointment, I finally got my mammogram results, and it said I was fine! It confused them, in the hospital, that my mammogram had shown nothing. I don't think they really believed me and said that tissue can feel like a lump. But then they did the jelly machine (ultrasound) thing, and they found it. They have put a tiny bit of metal, into the lump to mark where it is. That is me now on a "conveyor belt' of having to sign acceptance for things. It is all happening very quickly.

I told my work colleague, Diane, today. I also told my boss, as we were on a video call. I just told him that I had an appointment.

I want to wait for the results, don't want to tell my loved ones. I don't want to hurt them; it is so horrible. But I am wondering if also, I don't want to tell them as it makes it all real.

Now I have to wait until 19th July, slap bang in the middle of my holidays. I wait all year for my butterflies and don't want to miss any butterfly days. (I love to go walks and take photos of our beautiful natural world,)

When you live in Scotland, even although it is the summer, you also have to wait for the right weather for the butterflies.

There is a gap in the butterfly season. You get them earlier in the year then there is a quiet gap before they start to appear again later in the summer. Remember, that I am on the autistic spectrum, so things that are **very important** to me, may not seem so important to others.

I was stunned to find out that they didn't seem to have a proper record of my "'monster cyst' from back in 2011. (I will tell you more about that later.)

Last night I slept but then woke about 2am. I can still sleep; it is not real yet. It is like the "Five Stages of Grief" (*Kübler-Ross, 1969*), denial, anger, bargaining, depression and acceptance. You can go round and round the cycle not reaching the acceptance part.

There is not much I can do but wait and see. Cancer is interesting, no one wants to talk about it. Like death. I think we need to focus on the why, how and what, rather than destroy, poison and fight. It is just cells growing more than they should and then distorting.

There is a book that I have read a few times, *Dying to Be Me* (Anita Moorjani) about a lady's incredible journey through cancer. I wanted to give it to my best friend Babs, but I couldn't because of the things that she has gone through, I did not want to upset her. Also, because not everyone, in fact no one really, can do what Anita did. I must look up what happened to her (the author). Well, I looked it up and she is doing good and now I follow her online.

I wrote in my first two books, *Living Diagnosis* and *Answers Inside Out*, about my monster cyst and losing my job. Well, fifty jobs are to go at work again. All I can do is forget about it, for now. That is much easier to do now that I work from home.

I am a very spiritual person. I talk away to my loved ones in spirit. I am glad that I don't get seen or checked up on by medical people as they would probably think that was very strange and maybe even put me on medication. It is my way, and it really helps me to talk to them and have them in my life, even if it is in my head.

I don't want them to give me the treatment which is "poison", but I have worked out, that yes, it is bad for me but, of course, it is much worse to die. So, I will take it. But if the cancer is all through me, then I don't want any of the treatment.

I have been thinking of the different people that I will have to tell. It gets worse the more I think about it. My friends and family. I hadn't realised how bad that must have been for Babs (my best friend) to have to tell it, over and over, and tell people about Andrew (her brother who lost his own battle). (That is **not** my story to tell but I mention it as it was a massive event in their, and our, lives.)

Thinking about it, I can't see the point of things. It all seems not to matter. But I realise that I just have to enjoy life. Suddenly I think that I can't be bothered with photography but that is my life. It is funny and strange to think that I might stop that.

I could go out and paint but there is too much to carry. I could go out and write but I would miss so much when not looking at my beautiful world of nature.

I just have to love and look after myself. Allow and flow with my thoughts and feelings. I see more now, why men (generally) just want to be left on their own to deal with things. It is too much to think of other people's feelings, I have to deal with my own.

I am fit, well and healthy, why would I have cancer? I eat well, get plenty of fresh air, I don't drink or smoke. I don't have it. I just seem to get big cysts and lumps.

Why did they not have my monster cyst on record? What do they have? Do they know about my Aspergers (now called autism)?

I have done lots of wees today. I think that is because of the stress. I think that the discomfort that I get, in my side (have done since 2011 when I got my monster cyst), is maybe stress related.

I can't have my bath (because of having had the biopsy and marker put in) I love my baths. That is my therapy.

I got home and there was a butterfly on my front door. Magical. A really lovely sign for me.

(I love synchronicities – what some people might call coincidences – but they happen so often and get more magical as they go! I have a notebook in each room that I write my synchronicities down in. I had written, in my notes for this book, synchronicity, hug and car. I had no idea what that might have been, so I looked it up in my notebook to see if I could find it. It turns out to be a lovely one and very appropriate as I have just been telling you about Babs' brother Andrew.

I was walking up the road thinking all this and about Andrew, when I looked at a car number plate which had the letters HUG. I thought that was really nice, then three cars up the road, I looked at another number plate and it said HUG again! Now, how many car number plates have you ever noticed with the word hug on them? Thank you, Andrew, a brilliant synchronicity.)

I am tired. I woke up, about 4.30am, worried about Dad. I don't want to tell anyone yet but then he can't talk to people about it.

I am fine and then I get fed up, as I suddenly remember again.

I am looking into all the healthy eating. Giving myself healing, to change the cells back to normal. Cancer is just a word. It is that word that brings fear and terror. That, is not conducive to healing.

(My head jumps about all over the place, well that is how it seems to other people and writing up these notes is quite odd as it shows me just how much it really does jump about! But I am going to write it as these thoughts arose as that is the journey that I was going through. I will add notes and extra comments as I go along, using brackets.)

I am a very spiritual person, not religious but spiritual. I say my prayers every night. I don't think people believe me if I ever tell them that, but I do. My granny taught me to do that. It really helps me just before I go off to sleep.

I say things and people laugh as it is a strange thing to say but I say what I mean. They don't really know how to take me at times, so I think laughing is the easiest and best way to deal with that, for all of us. Laughter is the best form of medicine, and I am happy with that. I can say things wrong such as, "this room is stinking". What I really mean is that to me, who is extremely sensitive, that it bothers me and makes me feel ill. I don't mean it as an insult, it is nothing to do with the other person or people. Also, sometimes I can get my words wrong. I can be hurtful. That is very muddling to me, I never mean to be upsetting to them. I also, sometimes, say what people shouldn't say. Perhaps it is to do with the different sides of the brain again (read more about my thoughts on all this in my book, *Answers Inside Out*) but the things I say just come out, there is no sort of policing to it as it is what I am feeling in that instant.

(Well, now I am going to talk about something that is very difficult to talk about. It will not be nice for my close family to read about but it is something that I think is important to talk about, at least this once and in this book as it is a massive part of the whole story and journey. It is an extremely private thing to talk to you about and not something we ever talk about in my family but now it is time for me to do just that. These are just my memories and could be wrong or muddled, I was only six and I have never talked about them with anyone, as far as I know.)

I never talk about my mum dying when I was 6. But all this has made me think of such things and it is perhaps time that I did, talk about it some more. I remember my dad taking me to visit my mum in the hospital. I have a memory of him, on the way, teaching me how to say hospital and ambulance as I was not saying them correctly.

In the bedroom of our old house, I can remember mum showing me a pile of clothes that were for when we were going to go and live in France. I wonder how our lives would have been if that had happened. It must have been what mum and dad had planned for when mum got better. Dad said that they never talked about cancer. That was the way then, he was actually told not to mention it. Imagine that. Imagine being really ill and knowing or suspecting that you might be dying but not talking about it to anyone! I am so glad that society is very different nowadays.

The day she died, I had had the best day ever at school and to make it perfect, Dad came to pick us up. But it turned out that poor Dad had to tell us the worst news ever. I had no idea that my mum was going to die. I don't know if that was because I was young or just because I am me, but I didn't.

When we got home there were some family friends there. The youngest of the boys suggested that mum might just have gone out for a walk and would be back soon. I really hoped that was true but, sadly, it turned out not to be.

My brothers, and I, got to sleep in Dad and mum's big bed that night. I remember looking at the big family tree that was on the wall. Another family friend, Margaret, came in and spoke to us. I also remember being afraid of mum being a ghost.

It is strange for me to think of that now as I talk away to my loved ones, who have died, and I have no problem with the idea of spirits or the afterlife at all. However, this was all many years before I developed those beliefs, myself, in my adult life. I also remember a number of years later, after my Grampa had died. I went to my Granny's house. Granny and Grampa had twin beds. I had to sleep in Grampa's bed one time and for some reason, perhaps it was a last-minute visit, I had to wear Grampa's pyjamas. I remember being really worried about the ghost of grampa. It is so strange for me now to think of that as my beliefs have changed so much and I know how much my Grampa and mum would have and do love me and that they would still be the same person that they ever were. Anyway, I know that my beliefs are different from many others and that is how I felt, at the time, as a small child.

(I may sound a bit strange and young here, but it is a very strange thing for me to talk about. It has never been talked about and so I suppose I am still that small child when it comes to this subject, all these decades later. I am going to bed soon and I know that I will be worrying about having written this and whether I should have. I can feel my side, uncomfortable, already. Perhaps that is part of my autism. My mouth still gets dry in the evenings since my treatment although it is getting very much better now. However, it is worse again tonight. I am tired and have work tomorrow. But I know this is right and actually will be very therapeutic and cathartic for me.)

(Remember too that I have autism, that doesn't go away. It doesn't matter if I am 6 and no one knows that I have it, or if I am 56 and some people believe that it makes no difference. It is a part of me, how I process things and how I am.

Perhaps with this, my third book, people will begin to know and understand how the autistic spectrum colours my world. The way my books are written may not be the usual way, but they are my way. They illustrate just how my brain and mind work and process things. If that seems disjointed or muddled to you then that may be because you process and order things in a different way. It does not make one of us right and one of us wrong. What it does, is create a picture of how my world works. **For me** that is the right way. I never was one to follow a trend or rules and regulations just because that is the way that we are meant to do something.)

I can remember walking up the road with some other kid, later, I don't know when. There must have been an adult listening to us, but I don't think that they were with us. The kid asked me how my mum died, and I answered, "nobody knows how she died". The adult said, "yes they do". I think what must have happened was that I had heard that they didn't know what type of cancer it was and thought I had heard that they didn't know why she died. Although just typing this, here, I am thinking that perhaps I heard someone asking or saying why did she die or something like that. However, I think I had just picked it up wrong and thought that they didn't know what kind of cancer it was. I always believed that, but when asking Dad about it, recently, he said that what it was really, was that they never found the primary source of the cancer. I began to wonder about that as I have found out so much more about cancer now, but that is how I have understood it all that time. What I do know is that my mum had breast cancer.

A few years later, My Dad, oldest brother, Chris, and I, went to live, for a short time, in Sardinia. My Dad doing overseas work for the company that he worked for. We went to school there. It was one room with a big table. There were only four pupils. At break time I remember the teacher's dog chasing geckos and that is where I learned that a gecko can make its tail detach and then grow a new one, as a safety mechanism.

While we were there, my other brother, Duncan, went to stay with our Aunty and Uncle, in Kenya. When we got home Dad proposed to Sue and they married that same year.

I remember being back at our local school. I had a small leather bag on, which I had got in Sardinia. We all had to stand up and the teacher said, "lose the bag Blanche". An example of my autism there, I can remember the scene and those words from nearly 50 years ago. That same time, perhaps the same day, a kid or kids started teasing me saying, "poor Blanche, we have to be nice to her, cause her mum died!" I did not like that. There was a girl in my class called, Karen Mathews. Her brother had died. She came up and told them to leave me alone. I really appreciated that and was never bothered, in that way, again.

Back to synchronicities and the present. I went out to sit in the sun. I wanted to relax and do some thinking. I was sitting on the garden seat when two young men walked down the lane laughing and having fun. They were going to a house there but saw me and came into our garden. It turned out that they were helping Cancer Research. I have lived here many decades and have never had anyone doing that, visiting the flat. If I hadn't been sitting in the garden, then they would never have talked to me.

I let them do all their spiel. It was about new research that needed funding for a new kind of treatment for certain types of breast cancer that would not use chemotherapy. I said that I was really interested in finding out more about it and explained my situation. They were a bit put off their banter by that. However, they were really nice and gave me an internet link to find out more about the research. I realised that the research was too new to be helping me and found out, later, that it was for a different kind of breast cancer. But it was all really amazing that of all the people that ever enter our shared garden, it was them that day.

It was the day before my appointment for the results of the big scan. I was back at work after the holiday. My boss had a good chat with me on the video thing. I told Diane (my work colleague) that I was to have a chat with him. I laughed so much when she told me to tell him all about it and "get it off my chest"! We luckily both saw the funny side of that completely inappropriate comment, and the laughing really helped us both.

I am having good times, and then bad, when I know that I have to let them "poison" me. It is a rollercoaster of hope, giving up and acceptance.

See Salt Tears

The Big Scan

I knew that I had to get a big scan to find out if the cancer had gone deeper.

It is hard and strange to type the word cancer. I hope it doesn't put you off. We all have connections, trauma and bad feelings connected with such a thing and word. But to me it is important to realise that it is just a word. A word for a group of cells that have distorted, changed shape, grown and started to multiply.

To me, it is **not** the correct way to look at it as something to fight, destroy and eliminate. It seems that it would be better to look at the cells and work out why they have changed. What is your body trying to tell you by reproducing all these cells. Why do they change? Why do they grow? Why do they block things? What could be done to stop that happening? How could they be healed and encouraged to stop being stuck and building up?

However, I have it now and so I have to trust our brilliant NHS (National Health Service) to deal with it the way they do and hope that all goes well. Life is one big journey. I have had a wonderful life and journey. I would not ever choose this particular part of the journey but that is what I have been given and so I will just have to take it step by step, stay cheery and see if I can make the most of or maybe even enjoy the journey as much as I can. I have always been one to prefer my own bed and my own wee world, but I am on this journey so perhaps I can share it with you which will be very therapeutic for me and hopefully help some of you along any similar journeys or just as a learning and discovering experience.

My Dad has been brilliant throughout this journey I am so lucky to have him with me and all my friends and family. Dad had promised to take me to Dundee for the "big scan". Now, we just had to wait to see when it would be.

Surprisingly my doctor phoned up to say she had just got the letter about my original scan results. It was lovely to get the phone call. I don't think she was that interested in chatting away, but she was really nice, and it made me feel like I was back with my good old family doctor again who knew me and my history.

I still don't know what her name is. She says it quickly and my head doesn't process words that don't make much sense to me. It is in a way, like I can't hear them, although I do hear the sounds. I would have to make an effort to look up the doctor on the internet and read what her name is. I have done that a couple of times but still couldn't tell you what it is. I would have to make the effort to think about the name, process it, and then try to remember it. Or to hear it said a lot more, once I know what it actually is. I am telling you this as a matter of interest as this book is also about life with autism. It is hard, I would think, for people to know or understand these things happen to a perfectly fine, ordinary, intelligent person, so that is why, I believe, it is important to write and explain about them.

The doctor asked me if I had got my appointment for the scan yet. I told her I had not. A day or two after that, I got a phone call to tell me when my appointment would be.

It is terrifying, I don't want the scan, as that makes it real and I am terrified that it has spread all through me. I am thinking about my monster cyst that I had in 2011 and the pain or discomfort that I have had under my left rib since then.

I know that it is for the best.

Dad is not so confident with driving to Dundee now. We had a lovely time with Duncan here, on his wee holiday.

I have not been sleeping well, I think that is connected to the autism and, of course, worrying. When I was first told about the cancer, I did not sleep for two nights. I am doing much better now.

I slept well. I was up at 7.30 am. Far too early but was ready in good time. We had to work out the parking at the hospital. It was pouring. We took the wrong road and happened to see the unit that we were to go to.

I had to take all my jewellery off. I wear ear piercing studs which I never take off, except, once every few months to change them, I have a lot of them, all different colours. I also have a gold chain necklace with a small heart and dolphin on it, which I never take off.

Everyone is so lovely. They help me and lead me about, so I don't have to think. They very nicely went to tell dad that I would be about ½ hour.

I had got the appointment over the phone, so had not got a letter, and so, there was no leaflet to tell me what might happen nor how it would work. So, it was all unknown to me. But I had been in a scan machine before, for my cyst.

I couldn't work out how to tie the gown and, of course, the men were not meant to help me. But he just said that it didn't matter and so I just held it closed.

I was worried about my runny nose as I was to lie face down for the whole of the scan. I get allergies and often have a sniffy or runny nose, especially if my head is down the way.

The lady at the scan machine was really lovely. When I was told that I was to lie still, I said that I might get a fright and jump. I get really bad frights. She told me that I was over thinking things and I nearly cried. If I am trying not to cry, then I can do that for a long time, but it is when someone is nice that I might cry, as I then let my defences down.

How can I stay still for ½ hour?

I don't know how people do with the machine, there must be many who don't, and just can't cope with it, but it is for different reasons, different things for autism that we are worried about.

They got me to get on the bed thing, face down. Put ear plugs in and headphones on. Then got me comfy with cushion things.

I kept my eyes shut the whole time. The machine was very noisy. There was music playing through the headphones, I chose classical, to relax me.

A voice talked to me to ask how I was doing and test that I could hear them. I answered but must have been too quiet, so I answered again, and they said that they had heard me. A panic button was put in my hand which, of course, I was terrified of pressing by mistake! They said I was to press it if I had any troubles at all but that then we would have to start the scan all over again.

I didn't know if I could breathe deeply as I was not to move. I realised later, that was just my autistic worrying as of course I could breathe! But trying not to breathe deeply did not help!

Halfway through, the voice told me that the machine was going to give me the injection in two minutes. That terrified me. I hate waiting for something and not knowing what the injection would be like and from a machine, was not good!

I did fine! I actually quite liked it! I told Dad that, a few hours later, he laughed and couldn't believe it. I had come out of the scan, at the time, very dopey, shaky and dazed.

When we got outside, I was really shaky and couldn't breathe. Poor Dad must have got a fright. We got going home, I got settled, my breathing calmed down and I was soon doing well again.

I had, previously, arranged tea out at my favourite restaurant, Delivino, with my good friends, Helen and Dolores. Which I managed fine.

The Start of It All

16th July 2023: Oh dear, what a day! Yesterday I got home from a lovely day in the park with Babs to find a letter for an appointment. I read the date wrong. Luckily, I phoned Babs to tell her that I had got my appointment, to find out what is going to happen, and she asked if I was sure that it was that date, which was still quite a while away. I reread it and it turned out that it is today! Dad is away, so Sue is going to take me.

I am home now "There is so much we don't know about autism"! I am to get 6 months of chemo! No choice, although he (the oncologist) says that I can say no. I don't want these "poisons" put into me.

But I feel better now as I know that I have 3 weeks, so I can heal myself with my magic food. I feel they took all my chance at healing time away from me, now I have a chance for healing. I will then still eat healthy for the treatment.

He says that I will lose my hair. I am already looking up head wear for the wedding (Babs' daughter is getting married).

I will be off work for 6 months or more!

People know about my Aspergers (I know it is called Autistic Spectrum now, but this is how I still think of it, as that is the name that I always knew it by. I will get used to the name change soon enough. I mean no disrespect or upset to anyone by still using the name Aspergers). The oncologist asked if it was alright to let people know about it, as he felt it would help. It is very weird. I am not used to people knowing about it. I have lived so many decades of my life not knowing, myself, that I am on the autistic spectrum, that it is not something I ever really mention or bring up in a conversation with anybody.

Now that it is in my medical notes and the staff all seem to be aware of the fact. It is a strange thing to get used to. I am not used to my autism being taken seriously or even being known about. It feels like I am being treated as if I am a bit daft, at times, but it is also nice, refreshing and really helpful. I am glad that the oncologist suggested that he let people know.

Since then, I have had a good day out with my good friend Dolores. Laughter is the best medicine. We had a great blether. I have a bit of a headache now. It is all sinking in a bit more.

I don't know what I will be allowed to take with me for the treatment. I have looked it up in Google. I might bring my laptop in the bag with books and things.

We, Dolores and I, had a spiritual time, visiting the lovely and atmospheric, Fowlis Wester church. Fowlis Wester is a tiny village not far, in the car, from here. I have a beautiful photo, in my living room, which was in my photography exhibition, of one of the stained-glass windows from that church.

While we were sitting out, in the beautiful countryside, having our picnic, I got myself an incredible visit from a moth friend! It was really lovely and incredible, like I was giving it healing. It was white with some yellow in it. I gave it a bit of healing, on the path, and it flew up. I found out that it had landed on me. It then just stayed there! We had our lunch, and it was still there. After lunch I got up to go, and there was the moth, it had been sitting, peacefully, on me all that time. I was a bit worried about it, but it just flew off.

6am: I am writing when I should be sleeping. I just need the words and thoughts out of my head. I have the daftest set of words in the world: "Don't worry about it." and "How are you?" These words are just going round and round in my head, over and over.

Sue says not to keep calling the chemo, "poison." I have decided that it is like a Dr Who Regeneration. The machines regenerate me, and I will emerge a refreshed person.

6th August 2023: I was thinking about how if anything happens to me, I would like people to know what my special things are. I then read a paragraph in a book which said that love goes into all the special things that you collect in life.

18th August 2023: I have a 23mm lump, it is called triple negative breast cancer and is grade 3. Scarily, Grade 3 means that the cells, "look very different from normal cells". I am to get four treatments of Epirubicin and Cyclophosphamide chemotherapy, once every three weeks. Then I am to get twelve treatments of Carboplatin and Paclitaxel, given weekly.

I am to give myself an injection, on the day after the treatment, this is to help me fight off any infection as the treatment will reduce my white blood cells too which deal with infections.

I am also to get a genetic test to find out if it is genetic.

September 2023

1st September 2023: I started my chemo today.

There is a waiting room where the reception desk is, then, down a corridor, a second waiting room, the doors there, go into the chemo room. The treatment room has lots of big comfy, individual chairs, each has a chair table and a treatment machine.

You go into the room and up to the desk to say who you are and that you have arrived. The ladies (staff) are all lovely. There is a toilet there and you are told that you must close the lid before flushing as the chemicals, that they put into you, can cause people harm. They also tell you that your wee may be a red colour. I keep forgetting that and I got a fright!

They put a cannula in your arm, then attach a tube and connect you to the machine where you are monitored. The bags of treatment are hung on this machine and attached to you through the tube. They also put in certain medication to help, and you get washes put through too. The treatment bags are horrible to look at and think about, but it isn't sore or anything, and you can't really notice it.

We get given a drink and biscuit in the morning and the afternoon, although I don't take one, I just have my water. We also get given soup, a sandwich and a drink for lunch, which is great and very handy. The staff that give you the food are very lovely and help with opening the sandwiches if you need, as one hand is attached to the machine.

The machines beep away the whole time, there are a lot in the room, and they beep if anything is wrong, if the tube is not sitting right, if you move your arm too much, if they are not plugged in and the battery runs out and if a bag is empty or, when the machine thinks it is empty. The poor staff must hear all that beeping in their sleep.

Some people choose to have the cap things on their heads which might help stop their hair falling out so much. They are cold caps. They have that on and are also attached to a machine for that. I am glad that I did not choose to have that.

We go home with a bag of medication. I am to give myself an injection, tomorrow, in my tummy.

The day before my chemo the bottom of my ribs were sore, especially on the left-hand side. The evening of the chemo I was sore, both sides. The last couple of days I have been sore in the centre of my chest and on the lump just occasionally. I sometimes am getting piles a bit.

My tummy feels bloated. Should I keep the plaster on my hand for the whole day? For the first evening it feels like the time that I had sea sickness or heat stroke. I feel a bit better when I lie down.

2nd September 2023: My legs feel heavy. They are perhaps a bit swollen. I am sore above my left knee. My tummy feels bloated, and I do not want much to eat. Later, I phoned the helpline because the leaflet said to tell someone if feeling bloated and loss of appetite. I got through to a nurse in Dundee and she said that I should be fine.

I had two wee (urine) dribbles. (I have had trouble with wee dribbles since my monster cyst was removed, major surgery, back in 2011. It has got very much better, than it was, these last few years though. Until now, when I hardly ever have dribbles. Not a very good subject, but important in the whole subject of health for this book.)

Sue sat with me when I had to give myself the injection. I read all the instructions, and she helped me too. It was a strange thing to have to do but I seem, I hope, to have done it fine.

(It is so strange to be reading this back now as |I am typing it up. I was so worried and concerned about things and it was all so unknown to me. Hopefully this will help people that may be going through similar situations. It still makes me feel ill to type and think about the chemo (now more than a year later). I now remember and completely understand why I started calling it my, "Dr Who Regeneration". I just could not think about or say the word chemo.)

3rd September 2023: I had a wee dribble. I was feeling dizzy and sick earlier. I have no appetite but did eat each meal, a bit. I am feeling bloated again.

5th September 2023: Still bloated, when I eat, and uncomfortable in my side under my rib.

(I am uncomfy now under my left rib, typing this. More than a year later than the date that I wrote the notes. I do wonder if this is a stress thing?)

6^h September 2023: I am very burpy. I had the sore ear fold thing in the night. It is like my ear folds and stops the blood and I wake up very sore with it. (I still get this and have done the last few years, occasionally.)

The last two days I have noticed my piano sounding wrong. I read that the treatment can damage my hearing. I am wondering if there are any natural remedies that I am allowed to take that might help. How do I ask questions like these? I know I can phone but I know how incredibly busy they all are, and I don't want to be using up their valuable time.

8th September 2023: It was a heart scan today. The treatment can cause some damage to my heart, so they need to see how it is working.

I didn't like the waiting room. There was a huge, loud, television. All the chairs were in tight rows facing the tv. I tried to sit sideways so that I didn't have to look at it but that wasn't very comfy and must have looked a bit strange too. The tv was too loud, and I just couldn't switch off from it. If I looked at the subtitles, the words made me feel ill. I couldn't stop listening to it. I started writing my notes to try and switch off.

I had to come back to sit in the waiting room, after the first check up and injection, I didn't like the questions much. I like to ask questions, but the lady said I was to let her speak so that she could explain everything. That does not help me, as I like to ask and find out about things, to put my mind at ease. The torniquet thing that they used on my arm was like a rubber glove type material, it nipped and then pinged back on me. I bruise very easily just now, because of the treatment.

I then had to sit back in the waiting room for twenty minutes. Dad had gone away to the car to wait for a while as he hadn't known that I would be back in the middle. He couldn't switch off from the noise of the tv either.

My ears seemed a bit wrong on Tuesday. My piano and music didn't sound right. It seems to be getting much better now. They say that the treatment can permanently affect your ears. They also say that it can affect the pumping of your heart.

While waiting, someone came in and called a man's name. There was only one other person, a man, in the waiting room, we both looked at each other. He wasn't the man that they were looking for. I was wondering just how many people panic and don't turn up for scans and things.

My eyes have been bad since Thursday. On Wednesday evening, I couldn't read or do the computer. I couldn't see very well.

The big waiting room tv, just mentioned a rainbow diet. A good balanced diet is very important. I had stopped eating ham, but I reckon that I need some meat as I don't like pulse vegetables. Ham has nitrates and preservatives. But I have decided that I have to stop obsessing about such things. I am a fit, healthy, balanced person and look after myself very well. It is not something that I have done that has caused this.

I am so tired. My head is whizzing around like a Duracell bunny, but my body is going really slow. I needed to calm down, I write so many letters and this book, in my head, in the night. I just can't switch off. I am getting much better but any changes, set me back with each new thing.

This scan is called a Nuclear Medicine test of the heart! Not the most relaxing of names. The leaflet says, Welcome to the Nuclear Medicine Unit. It tells you how they will inject a small amount of radioactivity into you. So that, and because I hadn't had the scan before, did not help with my buzzing head.

I am still much more relaxed even although I can't sleep. Perhaps that is because of the steroids or the medication?

9th September 2023: I had to lie down after playing charades in one of our board games. It took a while for my heart to calm down. I have a sore mouth especially top right at the back. It is sore to open my mouth.

(Dad, and I, play a board game on a Saturday morning. I think the incident that I mention above might have been the hilarious time during a game of Cranium (*Cranium, Inc., 1998*). We have created our own version of the way to play, for this, and many of our other board games, so that we can play it with just two players.

It was my turn to act out the clue to try and get Dad to guess the answer which was, "streaker"! I tried to take it easy, but Dad doesn't always seem to get my acting! So, I was trying to gently run about the dining room, miming taking my clothes off along with playing a game of cricket! Anyway, it all turned out a bit too much for me, hence having to go and recover on the couch. It was hilarious though, to tell Sue why I had done too much.)

10th September 2023: My heart has been fluttery at times. I am feeling a million times better today (this is a week and two days after my first chemo). I have a very sore mouth. It is hard to open for eating. I got a thing that feels like the top of my thigh is going to dislocate. I carefully moved it correctly, but this happened a few times.

11th September 2023: I woke up with very sore lower ribs, at the back, on both sides. A wee bit dozy from doing fiddly proofing for work. I find myself tired when waiting in a queue at the shop. I have one of those burst blood vessels, underneath the surface, that I get on my fingers, but this one is on my toe.

I sent the big, long letter that I had written to the Oncologist. I sent it by email. Here is what I wrote:

Dear (the oncologist)

*Hello and thank you very much for all your amazing work generally and for the letter you sent to summarise our appointment. I realise that I am **very probably not meant** to write or disturb your busy, vital work with letters and will make sure not to make a habit of it! However, I have had many nights planning, when I should be sleeping, for hours, what I could say about this whole thing, both questions and points that I feel might just be **very important**. Please also excuse the length of all this but I have decided that it might be a very helpful and therapeutic thing for me to do.*

I am not so good at telling people things, nor thinking quickly enough to speak or ask about things. I am a million times better at writing them. I also noticed your amazing, genius, savant skill at looking at my scribbled questions on my paper and reading them, knowing what they were on about and answering them before I had even managed to read the first letter of them, and I wrote them! So, I reckon this might just work somehow or at the very least help me to explain things as I want to, a bit more.

I also realise that we can phone the chemo centre and the helpline any time. But it seems so wrong to phone the people in Perth just to ask about things that I am wondering about when they are so busy and have a massive room full of patients to take care of. You have all been so lovely. We are so incredibly lucky to have you all, and our NHS.

Yesterday, 7th September I had my genetics appointment. The lady, got me to understand it all a lot more and why I might actually want to know for my nieces etc and their own life choices and also about how it was the DNA (or whatever it is) going wrong, so that they can't do their job of protecting the breast and ovary cells and that is why it is okay to remove them, as then they won't then have that tissue to do that to. I was also asking her about the PARP inhibitors. I am really interested in that and whether, if it was to be genetic, that could be a different path to go down instead of the chemo? It makes so much more sense if it is a genetic reason and cause and also that it is 70% more likely, if you have the gene trouble, for that to have caused it. I know that I have looked after myself so well that it would all make a lot more sense. The surgeon (Consultant Oncoplastic Breast Surgeon), in Perth, had already told me it was not genetic when I first asked about the PARP treatment as a possible alternative.

I am to wait to get the results of the genetic test, of course, but if there was any way and any chance, whatsoever, of going some path apart from chemo, I **would love that so much**. *And* urgently **before any more treatments at all**. *The second one is on 22nd September.*

I realise that you want to see how the lump is responding to the treatment and that is also very important for future treatment. I also know you said I couldn't have another scan before the chemo and understand that and how much the scans cost. It does seem really important to **note** *that the mammogram (in this case) is no good for showing it anyway, indeed does not at all, and that it showed up very well on the ultrasound. I saw it myself! But also really important, I feel, to note that the lady doing the ultrasound, in Perth, took a photo and said she would keep that one as it showed it well. So, there should be a saved file of it to compare with any future ultrasounds if there was any possible chance of some other kind of treatment.*

From what I am picking up, it seems that this type of cancer can be very aggressive but also, that it seems to come back. I really can't see how my body could go through all this treatment and then just have to do it all over again.? Although, of course, I know it would and I can manage and cope with that, it would seem that it would be a lot better to just remove the lump and then see what happens, without the chemo also killing all my body and cells? Obviously, I know nothing whatsoever about any of this and am only able to write my feelings and questions on what I feel is a **vital matter**. *So, I will try and write them down.*

I really do feel that the luteolin foods work very well and that I was doing a lot of good with that before the chemo started. Is there no work or treatment at all with this?

*First of all, I am very lucky to be so fit and healthy to start with and realise that I will be able to cope with and deal with the chemo and get through this. It went in me fine and I was fine until the Friday evening. (It was my first chemo treatment on 1st September 2023.) So, it has been a week now. I am feeling much better today (8th September) and even have my appetite back, quite a lot, which really helps, so I can get healthy things into me and help myself to heal. But oh, my goodness, as I guessed I would be, I am so **extremely sensitive** to it all. I cannot believe, at all, how effected I am by **just one treatment**, and I presume it just gets worse and worse. I know, now, that I just have to learn all the things that might happen and find ways to deal with them and what works best to cope with them.*

The first night (Friday 1st September) I started to get really sick feeling and dizzy. This lasted for a number of days. On the Saturday, I managed to walk up to my dad's and indeed have tried to keep active all the time as I know that is so important. If I sat for long, I felt dizzy and if I lay down I did too. But I had a great day and the next, got my dad to drop me at a walk and come and get me later where I sat and watched nature and took photos. That did me the world of good too. My step mum helped check me giving myself the injection on Saturday, after lunch. That seemed to go fine. But I could not eat anything much before that. Then, teatime, I could not eat a thing. The food, even just a tiny bit of nuts or toast, just went round and round in my mouth and would not disappear, tasting of nothing whatsoever. My tummy got really bloated and I had no appetite at all. I even, after reading about it in the injection leaflet, and wondering and worrying, phoned the helpline. They were very nice and helpful and said it would be okay and just to phone if it got worse.

That first while, it actually felt like the only couple of times in my life that I have had seasickness or heat stroke. Oh, and my legs were very heavy right from when I first got home, for a few days, like I was wearing long metal boots.

    I also got dizzy or motion sick feeling as soon as I went in the car. Tuesday, I noticed my piano sounded strange and Wednesday it did, and I couldn't listen to my music. The nights, I have been so tired as I have been wide awake thinking things through. I have arranged with my workmate and boss that I can just switch the alarm off and go back to sleep, if I need to, so that is going to help a million as then I don't have to worry about it. I was saying to my boss that it was like I was a "Duracell Bunny" in my head, which was whirling round and round at an incredible speed, but my physical body had to do everything so slowly (like the collapsed, non-Duracell bunny!) and that the two **did not work together at all**. I could just not calm down. However, I have worked my Tues to Thurs this week and absolutely loved it. Then Wednesday evening, I got so fed up as I could not manage to use my computer game nor read my book at all. I just could not concentrate at all and was not interested. Thursday, my eyes went bad, and I found it hard to see so well. I couldn't read my book either but this time that was also because my eyes couldn't seem to see the text so well, it was just too small.

    It was interesting today, Saturday 9th September. I am doing very much better. I was up at my dad's and playing a board game. I was doing charades, and he couldn't get it, so I was moving about a bit. I had to stop and go lie down on the couch for quite a long time. My heart went funny. Afterwards I was interested to see that my eyes had gone bad again. I couldn't read or see writing nearly so well again. I realise that I have to take things much slower and that will be a learning curve, but I think it is **terrifying** and very alarming that **just one treatment** has had such a massive effect on me, even when generally feeling much better.

    This is not about me not being able to be ill or anything. I am a tough person and know I can cope with a lot. I also know that many thousands or millions of people have done too. This is about an extremely strong feeling that it is **no**t the right way for me. Don't worry I am not going to go off to some other country and try purely natural therapies. I am really trying to explain this feeling and my thoughts about it.

I have felt my body just like skin and nothing much else a lot, already, since the chemo, like when you have been really ill for ages and lost so much energy and weight.

On Tues and Wed, when my hearing appeared to go all wrong, I then read that there can be permanent hearing damage and there is nothing that can be done about that. I can, just not, take things, like that, which say "can't". I did look up natural help for ear damage and it said ginkgo biloba. I don't approve of supplements as I think things should be found naturally in foods but was prepared to try this if it might help. But then read that it is not allowed when having chemo. I notice that the cancer leaflets I have been given often say about natural therapies, but these always seem to be the same 2 paragraphs and don't really tell you anything at all. As I have said, I am a very natural person and have never really taken any medicine my whole life. Not even paracetamol etc. I really mean that but also realise that there are always times in life when we need to get the doctor to fix us and fix us properly. That is when I have taken the medicine, and it has done the job very well, mostly. However, I have also noticed that it is very often only short term and not a holistic long-term treatment. We don't seem to have the knack to explore, study etc the core of issues that might really help massively, in the long term, for the whole of society and the world.

My left pinkie and the finger next to it have been a bit numb this week. That also worries me that it could happen so quickly. My mouth has been very sore today (Saturday 9th September) particularly at the top right-hand side and sore to open my mouth to eat. Still the same or worse today, Sunday. (Now, Mon 11th, I have phoned the people in Perth and am getting to go down to the Crieff Health Centre this afternoon to have my mouth checked.)

I know there are many side-effects and have experienced quite a few of them. I realise that is all part of it and that it is all explained to us. But I am just completely utterly stunned how much just one treatment has affected me and I **never** want to have any more of it **ever,** never mind many for months that will just get worse and worse.

I realise that you don't need to hear or read about all this, but I just wanted to try and explain some of it and how I am feeling about it all. But I also have, for a long time now, been thinking about all the connections that might be very important. As I said, I don't think people really listen to or know what I am going on about a lot. I also don't think people realise that when I say something is really bad, that **it really is**! I would like to write down and let you know some of the connections that I think might just be really important, even although people, doctors etc might not think they are of any relevance or not part of their particular area to deal with. I believe that communication is the answer to most of the World's problems and who knows it might help, even with just one thing that has not been mentioned and may be really important.

Filling out the genetic test and talking to the lady in Genetics has made me think a lot about all this. My Grampa had lung cancer which spread to his back. I had not known the details of this, it was back in the 1970s. He did smoke all his life but finding out or thinking again about what happened to him, made me think about my back.

Don't worry I am not giving myself things that I don't have or being paranoid! I have had a sore back for quite a few years now. I didn't tell yourself or the Consultant Oncoplastic Breast Surgeon this as I kind of gave up, the last time I told a doctor, when I was asking about something else during a phone appointment. Please note that I never very often go to see doctors at all and have never much needed to. This doctor, as I tell people with a bit of a joke but very true, appeared to have a catchphrase of, "I am not unduly worried about that". I will not say who, as that would not be right and also, they will, of course, know what they are doing. But when

I yet again mentioned my back, he just told me that sore backs are very common things. So, I decided I better stop mentioning it.

*However, I have told the surgeon, and a lot of other doctors and nurses over the years, about the pain or discomfort under my left rib. I have had this since 2011 (the year I got my 15cm ovarian cyst removed). They have all felt the area and said that there is nothing there and I agree with them, but this does not alter that fact that there is **something not right** there and it has not been, for so long. My old family doctor, before he retired, did send me for an ultrasound (if that is the correct word, the one with the jelly) to Perth Royal Infirmary. That must have been a year or two after my major surgery in 2011. They said that it was fine and also that my kidneys were fine. I do remember the person who gave me the scan, at the time, saying that they couldn't tell deeper though.*

I have noticed, with the chemo, and obviously a swollen not working very well tummy, that this area, under my ribs, has been digging away at me, a lot, and it gets sore first when my tummy gets swollen from this treatment. But what I am thinking and have for a long time, is, that there is a ring, I will call it a "belt" area of different things, right around my body at the level of my lower left rib. The area, below my rib, kind of digs in and can be sore at the front or the back. I also sometimes wake up, especially recently, with a pain in that area but at the back, on both sides. I have always thought, going by this, that it might be kidney related. I also told you about a "wee" problem that I have had since 2011 as well. My old family doctor, before he retired, taught me about how my routines etc were telling me my bladder was full before it was, and I have worked hard on sorting that. It is so much easier to do this the last few years as I have been working from home. At the beginning of the week, after chemo, I had 3 dribbles and haven't had any for months.

It is now Sunday (10th September), I have been writing this for 3 days so it may jump about a bit! (Feeling a million times better today and have wanted and eaten my meals very well.

Still have had a bit fluttery heart at times.) Last night I got very burpy. I have been the same a bit today. I get that sometimes (perhaps stress related) but when I had my ovarian cyst, I was in agony at times and the burps seemed to help but were really bad. In the night, last night, I got what feels like a big bump in my throat going from left, under ear in my neck, to the right (not usually that wide) building up like a bubble or burp in the centre. I also had some burning coming up last night and a wee bit today. My biggest brother has talked about his acid reflux for many years (that may be stress related) but I was remembering that dad always said that mum had indigestion a lot and I remember there always being a packet of Bisodol in the house, that belonged to her. I am telling you about that as the burps, when I had my cyst, came from just below my lower left rib area that I have been telling you about.

So, that is the "belt" of things around my body at the area of the lower ribs. But I also have 2 slight lump spot things, just small and I don't think anything to worry about. I just put my witch hazel and Teatree cream on them, if I feel them, and they soon go away, or I forget about them but that is also around the same "belt". They are just small, but one is a wee bit sore to the touch if and when I notice it. Soon clears up though.

Then to my back. I have had, for quite a few years now, a sore back. It is also around this "belt" area. It is a million times better these days after a few treatments from a lady at the Natural Clinic who I have seen just occasionally, over a number of years. She has also completely "cured" my extremely sore shoulder that I had on the right-hand side. She does " Craniosacral Therapy, and Visceral techniques". This work has helped me so much and I appear to respond brilliantly to it. I realise I can't visit her while I have a lump nor chemo.

But my back was really bad. I can walk for hours fine but as soon as I stand still for a long time, taking photos, I get a really sore back. When it was really bad, I would try to walk away and nearly collapsed with it a number of times. It is not like a sore back which I have had a couple of times in life and understand. This was something very different. This sore back area is also in that "belt".

So, having rethought about it all, thinking of my Grampa, I thought it might be important to explain that all to you, even although it has never seemed to be of great importance to any doctor that I have told.

Another strange health issue that happened, while still working in the office, so before COVID. I got an extremely bad face infection. I thought it might be shingles, they said it did not show itself in the usual pattern of shingles. I do, now, have 3 or 4 white dot like scars on my face from it, which are just like chicken pox scars though. They said it was a bacterial infection on top of a viral infection. I was off work for 2 weeks and had to go to the health centre every day to get checked. It started later in one week but after going to a pharmacist, nurses etc, didn't get taken more seriously until the next week. I ended up with large, extremely sore "eruptions" in a line going from the top left side of my head right down in a diagonal line to the bottom right of my face. I had them, also, in my mouth, one, really bad, inside the top of my mouth. The one below my left eye was the one they were really worried about because of any danger to my sight. I tell you about this as it was another strange case that seemed to be odd to them, so just in case it is important in any way.

For a while now, months of this year, I have noticed when I lie flat on my back (I sleep on either side) in bed (which only happens if I fall asleep very quickly, so not very likely just now, an incredibly strange loud roaring noise that has woken me up. Now, I know that people snore, but this is an unusually loud noise. I also noticed that sometimes, in the same position, I would suddenly wake up with like a big bubble flying up the middle inside of me from my tummy up to my mouth and very nearly sick although not physically sick and not feeling sick at all. That has not happened for a month or 2 now but both things were very strange and definitely different and nothing that I have ever had before.

A more positive and perhaps very interesting side effect of the chemo seems to be that I am waking up without a blocked nose. I have had dust and cat allergies since a child when I was really bad with them. I also used to get many bleeding noses. I have learned many tricks over the years to cope with these allergies and they are so much better although avoidance is probably a big cure! However, I use Olbas oil, lavender gel, vapour rub etc a lot which really helps. Since the chemo started, every morning I have woken up with a clear nose. I have never had that for decades, if ever.

I hope you will see the funny side of the next comment but the next incredible effect (since the chemo) on me, is that I have had "nose bogies"! I have also never had them for decades and I mean never. Possibly an important and interesting thing is that I had 2 large ones, and they appeared to be a kind of an odd white spongy type stuff. I wonder if something has shifted or if this all is important in some way?

The other thing I am wondering about is that I see that the second lot of chemo you are giving me, does not mention breast and does mention ovary.

I know that it is too late to be worrying about such things now. But it seems incredible to me that I had a "monster" 15cm cyst which obviously surprised many of the medical people especially in that I didn't know I had it! Actually, I was in such agony with it that I had been sick with the pain on a number of occasions, off my work for a week with what I thought was a sick bug at one point and couldn't sit up even to look out of the hotel window at the sea on a short holiday (it was after that I went to see about it) but hadn't known that I had the massive cyst. My doctor could not believe that I never knew.

Anyway, it seems to me, that to have such a massive and unusual cyst in my ovaries, way back in 2011, and especially if this cancer has ovarian connections, that it would surely have been really important for them to look into why I had that and *whether it might cause more problems. This is another of the links that I feel may be very important. I was very surprised, when starting on all this cancer journey, that the cyst and the major surgery that I received for it, were not highlighted or even seem to be pointed out in my notes. I realise that notes are long and need examining to find things, but this seems incredibly important. Basically, I was sent home, then later got the stitches taken out and was able to always ask my doctor about it but nothing else ever happened about it. No future check-ups or anything. I suppose this was because it was not, thankfully cancer, but it all seems very odd. Especially with it having been so large, (life threatening apparently (at the time)). As a matter of possible interest: I got the major surgery in Dundee, and I remember saying that they could take a sample of the cyst for research. So, if such records are kept and connected with the patient in any way, then there should be a sample of or data about that cyst somewhere.*

So, I felt it was really important to write and explain all these things and connections just in case something, even small, might help to connect or understand things more and might actually be as important, as they have seemed to me.

Thank you so much for taking the time to read all this and I reiterate that I realise that it is probably very unencouraged to write like this, so, again, thank you very much for your time.

I realise and understand completely that no matter what, I still have a large cancer lump and that you need to get rid of that. But if there is any way, whatsoever, to do this safely, without the chemo, I really would jump at it. It just does not, in any way, work right with me even although I am so lucky to be so fit, well, healthy, and able to deal with it all so much more than many other people who are not so lucky as me.

Yours sincerely

Blanche Haddow

That is an example of the sort of things that go through and round and round my head, especially when I should and need to be sleeping.

13th September 2023: Well, I wished that I had not sent that blooming email, as I often do, after I have sent it. I was contacted by the lady at Dundee saying that the oncologist would like me to go in to see him and discuss all the things that I had been asking and thinking about. I tried to say I didn't want to and that I wished I hadn't sent it. In the end, I agreed to go in, it was today.

He, the oncologist, was really nice. It was really good and nice of him to take the time out of his busy work to talk to me and go through all my worries. He had the letter printed out and went through it, bit by bit.

There were two other people in the room with us. At the time I wondered if that might be because I had made such a fuss, but I expect that they were trainees. He is a **very busy** man with an incredibly important and worthwhile job. I felt really bad taking up their time. But they were all really lovely, helpful and friendly.

He answered everything and said in one bit, I think you were just working this all out in your head. He is a really clever man and, also has a great sense of humour which really helps. He lets me ask all the questions that I want and, also answers them, which I really like.

I asked him about the wee black bit on the sole of my foot. He looked at it for me. He said that it was best to leave it to work its own way out by nature. I apologised for having smelly feet as I had been on a long car journey and was roasting. He replied that he had children and that smelly feet were the least of his worries! I also asked him to excuse my hairy toes! He said that was a great sign as it meant that my toes still had a good blood supply getting to them.

He also joked that he would get people to call him the GAS man now, as I had, in my letter, mentioned his Genius Savant reading skills!

It was so nice of him to take the time to do all this and to help me put my mind at ease, as much as it can be without anything actually changing. (He also sent me a letter about the appointment and all that we had discussed. They, the specialists, have all done this over the whole of this journey and it is a really nice touch that I greatly appreciate. We are so lucky to have our NHS.)

He did say, after all that, that he was happy to help but perhaps not to send seven-page long letters too often! I never did that again. It was just weeks and months of thoughts, fear, anger, frustration, etc all coming out in that one letter. It certainly was therapeutic and helpful for me to get it all out of my system. He put me right on some of my misunderstandings and thoughts and explained other things, why they happen that way etc.

20th September 2023: (I am not actually sure if this it the correct date for this as I haven't written the date in my notes. But I do know that it was the day I gave blood, that I had started chemo and that my hair was coming out a lot, so I think it must have been this date.)

I was down at the Health Centre to give blood. I wore my B Happy cap that I created from my photos of a bee and some flowers.

My hair is coming out loads now.

I got back from the Health Centre to see my phone flashing with a message. The Perth ladies had phoned three times. I am to go to Dundee about my fluttery heart. I phoned Babs who said Graham (her husband) would take me through if I couldn't get Dad. Dad took me through.

There was a big wasp in the car. I think that it might have

been a queen. It was moving, slowly, along the dashboard. I managed to get it out of the window.

I had got told that we were to park at the A&E (Accident and Emergency) bit. Then go in the door there, which is near to the chemo day care bit.

I had to give blood three times (I had also given blood in the morning) and get two ECGs (Electrocardiogram, to test the heart).

Dad went off for a walk round and to the car for a bit. I got given a wee lunch of a turkey sandwich, tomato soup and yoghurt. That was great as we had left in such a hurry, and I had not known how long we would be. I did not bring any food, water or anything and nothing to do. I talked to Dad for a bit, he bought me a crossword puzzle book thing, and I watched the busy room, patients and staff. Everyone was really ill. I felt a bit strange being there, still with my hair. It was coming out a lot though, I kept having to make a wee pile of it at the edge of the seat table. Each time they came over, they took some more of it away for me. I kept apologising about it but the man, very nicely, said don't apologise, we are doing that to you.

I had to wee in a sample bowl thing and leave it in the toilet shelf for them to check.

They were lovely people. All the tests showed that I was fine. I reckon that it must have just been from the treatment and also a bit of a panic. The lady did say that she had to do a test that she did not think would show anything, but it did, it showed that there was some enzyme or something working too much. She seemed surprised about it, but I never heard anything more about that.

We were in there for the whole day. We didn't get home until after 6 pm.

22nd September 2023: There was a wasp in the car today and another one on me when I got out the car getting home from Perth.

I realised that I had left my bag of medicine in Perth. I didn't know what to do. I phoned Babs to see if Graham would be able to pick it up on his way home from work. Then worked out that the lady at reception lives near Dad. So, I phoned and asked if she might, bring it home with her from work and leave it at Dads. She very nicely did. Dad then brought it down for me so that I had my medicine to take tonight.

23rd September 2023: I was sick in my mouth in the night.

(I am sorry to mention such horrible things. I hate even that word, never mind thinking of it, but I believe that it is important for me to tell you about all these things as they are part of this journey, and it is a journey about health. I find it incredible to read back these notes and find out how much the treatment affected me so quickly.) I expect I will stop writing such details in a while as I get further into the treatment. We shall see.)

24th September 2023: Since Friday, it is now Sunday, I have had a bit of a vein showing up my left arm. It feels a bit bruised and perhaps a wee bit swollen. My ears were pounding in the night.

25th September 2023: I still can't eat too much. It looks like a period might be starting. I only had one, last May, then in November 2022 before that.

I was out for my walk round with my cap on. I walked through the old St Michaels church hall gardens. I could hear people asking about who owned a dog that was walking around, out on the road. As I came out the gate of the gardens, I saw that one of the people talking was the man that I sometimes meet and say hello to on Lady Mary's Walk. He looked over towards me and said, "there's a man there", talking about me, to the other person. He then shouted over to me, "is this your dog?". I just looked at him, said, "no" and scuttled off. I suppose I must look like a young man with my cap and baldy heed (my Scottish, jokey words, for a bald head). But it was not very good for my morale.

26th September 2023: I have wobbly, heavy legs. I do have my period, the last thing I am needing. I thought all that was finished with. My poor body must just be wondering what on earth is happening to it.

28th September 2023: I have to go to sleep about 9.30pm. I woke at 3.30am, too sore in my ribs. I had to put the heating on yesterday as my neck was cold but then I was far too hot in the night.

I am feeling yucky today. My neck and ears were freezing, so I put the snood that I bought on. (I bought a couple of snoods to keep me warm during this, not something that I would ever have chosen to wear before or after this. For those of you, like me, who didn't know what that is, it is a circle of warm material that you can wear like a scarf and pull up over your head or ears. I think many more of us found out about them during Covid, when mask wearing became a must.) The snood makes me look like nun or an alien! (See a photo of me with it on in the timelapse video in my *See Salt Tears* website.)

I tried beef olives for tea to give me some iron. It seemed to help. I had not had any red meat for a while.

29th September 2023: My legs are a wee bit numb and heavy feeling, especially the top left.

October 2023

2ⁿᵈ October 2023: There seems to be two lumps or spots in a private place! Perhaps they are insect bites?

I went to drain the pasta, all ready to eat my tea tonight, and there was the pasta, still sitting, uncooked, on the worktop.

3ʳᵈ October 2023: I got the letter with the results of the genetic test, and they say that it is **not genetic.** I found the genetic thing really interesting. I used to love genetics in Biology, at school. The lady who talked to me about it all, was really interesting. I would have loved to talk to her more about genetics and all the autism side of things but of course that was nothing to do with this, so I didn't.

8ʰ October 2023: I am beginning to look less like the Fairy Liquid Baby and more like the toy, that you used to get, where the plasticine hair grew out of it for cutting with toy scissors!

I wish that I could just have my "baldy heed". It is annoying wearing a hat, especially with a hood. I need it for when I go in a shop as it would not be polite to go into a shop with my hood still up. It is only for society although I do also need it to keep me warm. I saw a clip, on Facebook, of a lady from Strictly Come Dancing (I think) who took her wig off on live tv to show her bald head. Why should people have to wear a wig? There is another famous lady who doesn't. I like and admire that.

Mind you I also need my hat, if it's sunny, as I am not to get sunburnt (as again I can't heal, I am, apparently, much more sensitive because of the treatment and I don't have any hair, including body hair, to act as a layer of protection).

9th October 2023: Generally, I am doing great, but I am extremely tired, especially from late afternoon onwards. I was sick in my mouth again. My leg has a sore area, top left, and I am itchy.

11th October 2023: I'm feeling fed up, I had a cry today. I got a lovely card from Jane, a family friend, today. She has been so lovely to me for decades. I had a brilliant day out with my good friend, Dolores, yesterday, Tuesday, it was a holiday from work.

I've been so tired since Monday afternoon. Dad phoned on Monday when I was making my tea. He thought that I was calling him on Facebook. He got a bit grumpy when I said I wasn't, as he said that he could see my name and that it was ringing. I was making my tea so was nowhere near the computer.

I have my routines and get slightly grumpy when they are disturbed but no one usually notices. (That is in normal times.) But now, I am so tired. Then he said, at the end, that Sue had seen it and, "I am not daft", or something like that. Usually, I would be calm, but I am so tired, and I never did like someone saying I was doing or saying something that I wasn't. So, again, I grumped that I hadn't said that he was daft, which I hadn't. This is an autistic thing; I don't ever want to hurt anyone and do not like when someone thinks that I have. (My autism is so much more intensified by all this.)

On Monday night I didn't sleep, even although I am so tired. I was trying to think where to go with Dolores. Then about what to say on Thursday 19th for the work meeting with two management people, as work is getting rid of staff again. Then thinking about banks and how they could sort things etc. I can't remember it all now, but I planned all that I wanted to say. Don't close the local banks. Give us personal people to talk to, even if it is online, that actually know us. The people, in my local bank, knew me, many of them. I had been with them for decades etc.

Then I had a brilliant day on Tuesday. On Wednesday I was back to work. It is so great that I work from home now. It is so much more easier. I am still so tired. Diane was having a day, nothing to do with me. She had said **many** times that we were off on Tuesday. I forgot, many times! It is like I know something but then say something else and that fact is gone. I know it, but it doesn't move over to the next thing that I say. I am just so tired, and they say that the chemo can muddle the brain. There is also the autism. I wonder if this is what Dad feels like all the time, having to make so much more effort to think about things and concentrate. It is like I need help, but I am **not** stupid.

I made quite a few mistakes today. I sent an email before it was finished. The internet kept stopping working. I had to go and give blood for my next treatment. I was frustrated about a Procedure and work, so I called Diane but had forgotten, again, that it was Wednesday and that she was in the office (She works at home some days and in work others). There she was, on the video call, ready to go to HR (Human Resources) about the Procedure. She laughed when I tried to say what I was thinking about it and the changes that they were planning. I know she was having a bad day and did not have time for me calling and, trying to change things, but I was getting all muddled up. I was trying really hard to stay calm and not mind at not having been asked about it all. I think someone else was there in the office. I told myself that it was not important, but I was left feeling confused. Should I just not say what I think and feel? The "Being not Doing" idea is great but is it right? Is it right for me to just do my own thing and never say what I think or feel? I feel so lonely.

(I wrote that, as it was in my notes and how I was feeling at that particular moment. Diane has been so wonderful and brilliant. She is a brilliant work colleague. She also deserves a medal for being with me, throughout the whole of this journey, both in a work capacity and, also in a listening and caring one too. But that day, things were obviously getting too much for me and that is why I am carrying on with typing up these notes, as they show the muddle and state that I was getting in. It is important to illustrate the whole of this journey, its ups and downs.)

People ask how I am but if I tell them, then they just don't want to know, or go on about being positive etc. We all do that, I think. There is a terrible fear about illness, death and cancer. I was the same before and had no idea that I was. We are still the same person. I hear people telling me things and giving me advice. Now, I see it from the other side. I understand, I too just wanted to help and didn't know how. But it means that I can't really talk to people.

Also, I have no one to talk to. I talk to Diane so much as she is the only one there, on a workday. It is obviously far too much for her and I don't realise. She has me, every workday, going on. All of them ask, how are you, but it was so much easier when I could just say, "lovely jubbly". That made people laugh. I liked that and it got rid of that horrible question. That is an autistic thing that I have read about in SWAN (Scottish Women's Autism Network), not liking or knowing how to answer or deal with the question, "how are you". Now, I just say, "okay dokey" and I don't meet their eyes. But now it is different as they see my hats and know that something is wrong. I like the people who just talk to me like normal.

I shouldn't really be writing all this now as I am so tired. It is 9.20pm and I will have to get to sleep soon. If I stop now, then it will still all be in my head. I have not read my book to calm me. But if I carry on. then my head will be working more. No one to talk to. Everyone is so lovely. A partner might be good. But it must be so stressful as you are stuck with them. They would be so sad, scared, worried etc. It may just be the same as it is with the people that I have now, Dad, Diane etc. Oh, I am so tired, and I am getting uncomfy from sitting here, in bed, writing. I am unused to writing. I am so used to typing.

I wanted to say so much more about today, but I need to read my book now, for half an hour, if my eyes stay open. Babs has had it so much worse, in hospital, major surgery, during Covid with no visitors etc and her brother Andrew too.

It must be so horrible for my loved ones. They want to be happy, cheery, get on with their lives. I don't want them to be sad, ill, miserable. Oh, I have to stop this, now, too tired. I love me ♥.

I am scared to leave this notebook and pen in the room tonight as I may wake up and want to write more. But if I put it in the other room, then I would be thinking about it. That is autism again. I don't think people without autism will know what I am going on about. People with it will, but will they ever read it? I don't want to hurt loved ones. That is what my other books seemed to do.

(Oh my goodness I am really pouring out my heart here! It is not like me. Never mind it was what I needed to write at the time so I will leave it in.)

Oh dear, it is 9.30 pm now and I am going to have to go to sleep without having read my book and my head is full of this. I have the pain in my left side now. Well hopefully I am so tired that I will sleep and switch off.

I have a bad headache. I will try some lavender oil on my pillow. Babs and Graham have not slept for years. I don't know how they do that at all. I'm bad in usual times if I even miss an hour. I just put the light out and now I am back already! My hand is sore from writing. I think I don't want to go to sleep as it is my third chemo, Dr Who Regeneration, on Friday.

13th October 2023: My third chemo treatment today. My legs are heavy. I have sore fingertips, two on the left and one on the right. I bashed my right hand. It is okay, but I put my lavender gel on it. (They say that because our white blood cells get killed off too, that we have to be very careful as we won't heal well. So, we have to avoid cuts, bumps etc.) I am feeling a bit sick and headachy.

In the night I had to use my big cushion as I couldn't lie flat for feeling sick. I couldn't switch off. I had to move very slowly when changing sides.

14th October 2023: Feeling yucky. I do not have much of an appetite, I could eat but then had to stop. I am dizzy and feeling sick. Feeling heavy and slow but I walked to Dads. That is a good thing for me to do. It is important for me to get fresh air and exercise.

15th October 2023: Wobbly, wobbly and very slow but I have had a lovely day in the park. I have no appetite.

In the night I was awake, sorting out the world. I heard a car door shutting and thought that was strange then realised that it was 10 to 5 in the morning, and I had still not been to sleep. I thought that I would sleep in but felt like getting up. I think I better do things naturally. I think it might be the steroids. (They give you steroids alongside the chemo to help you counterbalance the effects.)

17th October 2023: I did too much at work, working on the feedback video in response to, yet again, losing our jobs. I spent the whole day on it, and it did not work. I worked on, until 5pm. I was so tired that I couldn't talk right to Dad, Sue and Duncan on the phone. I don't think that they knew. I had tea, still not done a poo. I will have to go and get something to help tomorrow from the chemist if nothing has happened. I don't want to, that is not natural. I am so tired that I will have to go to bed.

18th October 2023: Went to bed at 7.30pm, I woke up at 10.30pm managed a bit of a poo but not right. I slept until morning and was up for work. I saw a red kite in the sky above the garden today. Brilliant to see one. I am ready to phone Perth. I am feeling okay, perhaps a bit dizzy. I ate breakfast but not wanting it. Finally done poo! It is Wednesday morning so that is since before Friday. That is me sorted, hopefully. I reckon that I did too much with my head, doing the video for work. I couldn't think or talk, but I just have to learn, work out and get to know about these things for now. I also had no sleep, Monday and Tuesday.

19th October: We had our work meeting, trying to tell them why we should keep our jobs. I have gone to sleep at 7.30pm the last three nights.

20th October 2023: I am a million times better today. I finally did a proper poo! I have very slow, wobbly legs and had a bleeding nose.

21st October 2023: I had a wonderful walk today ([21st October 2023](#)). The magic was a bit lost as I was watching out for humans so that I could put my hat back on before they saw my baldy heed. It was too hot but also too cold. I left my hat off one time when some people were going past. They said hello, but didn't even look at me. I saw me, in the mirror, when I got home, and I understand now, I look very weird.

I phoned home at the end of my walk, when I reached the concrete streets, to get a lift up the road. It turned out that Dad's phone had been pulled out of the wall, by mistake, so they never heard it ringing. It took me an hour to get home. I have to walk so slowly it is such a waste of my walk time.

It is so sad that some of the magic was gone. It was beautiful but I only got a few photos (that is by my standards, I can take over 100 photos on a walk in good times). I had a wonderful, magical time but in normal times, I think it is my autism that gives me the skill to get lost in my magic zone where time disappears. Now, it is like my head has two parts. It is a strange state that the treatment seems to be causing. I have a pain in my left ribs.

Dad was lovely and dropped me off for my walk. But I couldn't talk to him as I was still buzzing from yesterday, I was awake from 3 to 6am. Dad wanted to know the date for my new chemo but that makes me feel so ill, thinking about it. Then he was upset, he didn't show it, but I saw tears. I didn't want him to drive when he was upset, I was too tired to talk but he wanted to say to me about mum. I couldn't have that conversation then. Even although I knew Dad needed to talk about it.

So, I went off on my walk thinking about it all, instead of being in my magic place. When I got home, he said that their phone had been off. He and Sue must have had a grump or been upset. He said that she wouldn't talk about it with him either. She forgot that I had given them pastries yesterday. I know that it is getting to a time when I need to look after them both, but I can only look after me, just now. They are being so brilliant with me. But it is all so stressful on top of all I am going through. I know that I have to sleep tonight. I know that there is no need for stress, but I just can't switch off. My thumbs rub together and then I know that means that I won't be able to switch off.

I am ready to see Dad tomorrow and listen to him, about mum. I know that this is terrible for him and that, just now, everything is about me but that is all I can do just now. He knows that, but that does not help me as I don't want to upset him.

I will do my best to, "stop, listen and think" (that is my special mantra, the last few years, to help me in life) tomorrow when I see him. What they will have to do is trust me. If I "give up", then that is **my** choice. It is a positive decision about my life, death and treatment. It is hard for others as they don't see the belief in life and the afterlife that I have and know. If I stop chemo, then that is my choice, even if it kills me. If I am dying and choose to die, then that is my choice and wonderful. I don't plan to, but it would be so much easier if people could know, see and understand all this. I plan to live until I am over 100. I will just try to sleep tonight, listen to Dad tomorrow and then, if I can and am able, try to let him know my views.

22nd October: I have a very strange head; time seems all wrong. Apart from that, I am perfectly fine.

23rd October 2023: I had a good talk with Dad. He thinks that mum maybe didn't know that it was the chemo that was making her ill and that she thought that it was the cancer.

I don't want chemo as it is poison. I don't want that as it is so bad for me and kills me. **But**, if I stopped it, I might die. If I died, then the poison wouldn't matter. But I might not die then it would have been the right thing to do as the "poison" is what kept me alive.

Amazon seemed to say that my books had been bought by someone in US a week or two ago. But it doesn't seem to show in the graph. They are eBooks. Maybe eBooks don't show until they are read? But I think that they do. Anyway, I just thought that it is amazing to think that someone, somewhere, right now, might be reading and so immersed in the words that I wrote. So, I sent them a symbol. I wonder if it will reach them. My head has sent it. It is a rainbow with a gold key and the key has a charm bee on it. I thought to "say" what that means but then decided that it is up to them to work out what they feel it means. If I remember, then I will write this in my next book. (I didn't remember this but did find it in my notebook, so, here it is!)

24th October 2023: I got up for work this morning, well and hunky dory. I went a walk with Babs at lunchtime and realised that I am in a very strange state. In my head, I was saving before I did anything, crossing the road etc. (I do this a lot when using the computer, but this was when I was outside and no computer in sight!) In the shop I found it very hard to use my bank and club cards. I wanted to save at each step. I don't think anyone would know that this was all going on in my head at the time.

Now I am feeling fine and ready to get on with my work again. But I realise that something is far wrong, so I thought I better call the staff at the chemo room. I called them and they said it is maybe dehydration or blood sugar levels.

I was trying to save again in my head, when speaking to the lady on the phone, each time that I said anything.

It seems to be when I am talking to someone. I am fine apart from that. I felt like I was in a tunnel, in my head, after that.

Time is going wonky too. Slow and fast.

It is weird, after all that, Babs and Diane had no idea that that was all going on. Diane said it was just the last sentence of my email that worried her.

I have searched for and found that email. Here is what I wrote:

"I just gave Babs a phone there as she must have got such a fright from me today. I have told her that I am just going to carry on working, for this week, and see how it goes and that I will phone Perth straight away tomorrow etc if anything gets worse. I also said that you, would know if you hadn't heard from me for 2 hours or whatever in a day, that something was wrong.

I of course may be very late tomorrow morning, if I am feeling wonky, but you know this. I am actually trying to type this, and it is like typing in a tunnel."

26th October 2023: I have had the strangest most wonderful day. I had a great time at work. There were many synchronicities. Management seems to be saying, in an email, that we won't be losing our jobs. I also seem to be winning all my *Magic the Gathering* computer games tonight.

(I love synchronicities. It all started quite a few years ago when I started seeing numbers like 11.11, everywhere. These grew and developed over the years. Until now when I often hear words on my music or the tv that are just what I am thinking, or looking at on the computer etc. I have a wee notebook in each room in which I mark down my synchronicities. I always used to say thank you to the "angels" for them. Don't stop reading if you don't believe in such things, just know that this is a big part of my magical and spiritual life. They make me smile and happy. One day I will write a spiritual book about my experiences with such things.)

27th October 2023: Back to being a bit slow and wibbly wobbly this morning. My knees are a wee bit sore when walking. I am feeling slightly yucky.

30th October 2023: I woke up to seeing a lovely grey bird messenger this morning.

A grey, fluffy bird flew down to give me a message, in my head, as I woke up this morning. It was telling me that they love me. I am the Earth One. I am to have trust and faith. I am going to live until I am over 100. They love me very much; it is just their way (the birds) that they seem afraid. They love that I let them be themselves. I am not to worry about the time and spending it on others. I will always have the time, no matter what. I just have to have trust and faith. The hours thinking in the night are **not** bad, I would be tired anyway and this is giving me the extra time that I am needing. It was a lovely grey coloured bird, about the size of a robin or sparrow.

I keep having to go to sleep early, about 9.30pm or so, often, and three times at 7.30pm, which means I have even less time to do things. I am missing my reading time; my eyes get too tired. I know many people don't have time to or don't want to read but it is my medicine. It is like missing your tv, sport, wine, coffee, chat or whatever things that you love, in **your** life.

I find it fascinating the differences in my lifetime, looking through an autistic lens. For example, when I was studying, I was not able to read a textbook etc. I just could not take it in. I tried but would never get past much more than a page and did not take any of it in, at all. It made learning, studying and taking part in discussions so much harder. Things are so incredible now, with technology, that people won't know about this massive difference, unless we write or talk about our own experiences, as they were then. I have been thinking about the world, before we used computers. To spell something, we had to look it up in a dictionary. When I asked how to spell something, people would say, "look it up". I often couldn't as I didn't know how to spell it. What a stupid thing to say to someone. If I knew how to spell it, then I wouldn't have to look it up, especially when I had no idea how to start the spelling of the word.

The music, that I was listening to, said "wouldn't", three times there, when I had just typed it. I love synchronicities. I suppose that might be an autistic pattern thing, as it is a magic pattern. Find out more about my love of synchronicities on my website page (Synchronicity).

There is so much we don't know about autism. (My writing is really bad here, in my notes. I was obviously very tired but wanting to write down my thoughts. Things like fro for for and doos for does.) I can't really work out some of my writing or what I am trying to say in it, but I think I am saying that understanding our differences is why the books that we write now, about our experiences, will be so important for future society and understanding. As technology has changed so much in my lifetime and some of the particular difficulties that I had in the past, would not happen now and won't be known about, unless we tell our stories.

Don't try to "fix" us. We are all one. Perhaps that is an ideal, but it does not mean that All is lifeless. We are all different. It is that very difference, that is causing troubles, and it is fascinating that we are trying to make laws which say we are all the same. Obviously, I don't know from other point of views, but I expect that what people want, is to be allowed to be themselves, not to have all of us say that we are the same as them. That would not be empathy nor understanding, it would be, again, pretending that nothing exists, and nothing is different. Political correctness about whatever, including autism, is often, I feel, about fear, money, power. I certainly don't think people with autism (please note here that I am talking about what used to be called Aspergers), were involved in the change or loss of the name and whole category of Aspergers. Or if they were, then I think that they were not listened to, or perhaps not understood. Also, that they might be confused about it all and not want to do anything wrong.

Autistic people are very sensitive and notice things much more and quicker than others, I presume. But also, perhaps when things are much worse, then, they don't know when to say so, as they are so used to things being extreme, they are so used to that. (I have missed some bits of this. I have written what I could make out or work out, from what I had written as it was obviously very important to me. I think it was all about my thoughts about how we should have **changed** the name for Aspergers and **not** lost the whole thing, as if it never existed.)

(I am going to include these thoughts, words and ideas that I wrote down when in a strange state, often in the middle of the night, when already extremely tired. They don't always make sense, and it can be very hard to make out my handwriting which will add to some of it not making much sense. However, this is a story about the whole of my journey and having a strange head, and being in a strange state was a big part of the experience. So, I am going to include them.)

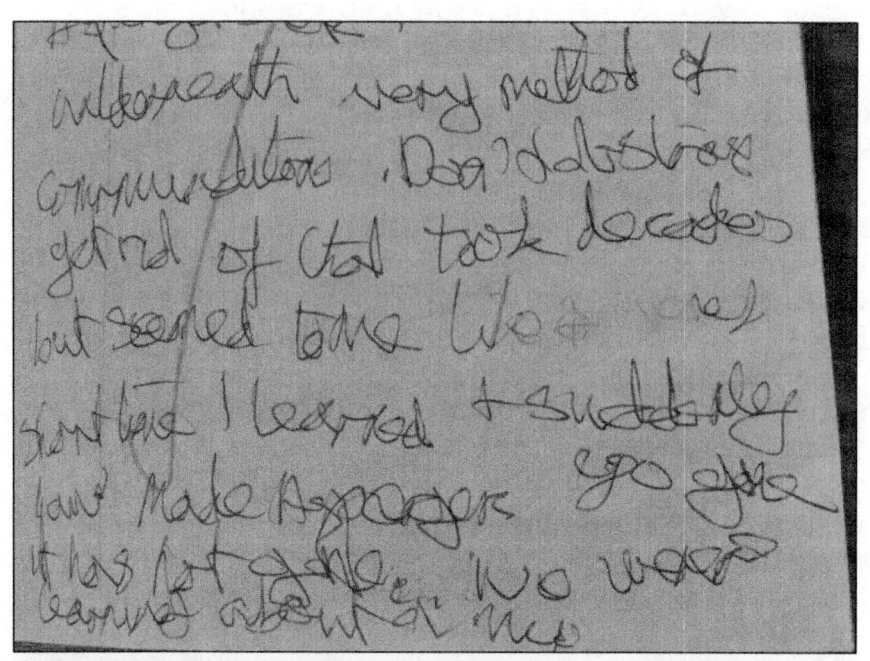

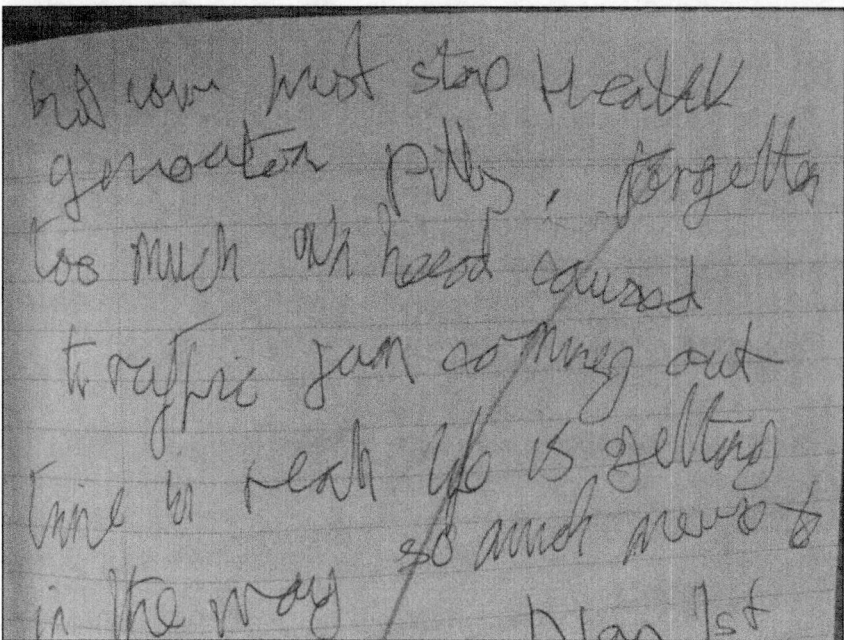

Examples of my handwriting when in a strange state and very tired.

We need to redress the balance with nature. We have had millions of years to begin to work out what is missing in the balance of humans, so now we have to create that exactly for us to see and we still can't see it. We see the terror and fear instead of loving, caring and understanding. We attack, fear and destroy. It is fascinating. Everything that's ever been, thought, feeling, idea is a lesson for us. There are many very intelligent people who are missing wisdom.

Maybe Ai (Artificial Intelligence) is the answer. Political correctness is wrong, it is the feeling and being, that matters, not the word. We could teach Ai to care; love and **I can do**. It is time for my things. I am missing all that with my head as it is and having no time, with what is happening. People are all so caring. But I have to be me and have to have trust and faith. I care so much; people don't get that.

I then, go on to talk about the stones of Machu Picchu, primary school building, and Roman roads. I don't know what I was talking about! But I suspect it would have been about learning from the past. How the most incredible work and buildings lasted. They were made to last. Our high school was built when Babs' brother was a baby as there is a photo of him with the school being built in the background. But that school has already been knocked down, in our lifetime. The primary school has been rebuilt too, but the old primary school building is still there and was built to last. It is stupid to build things that won't last, to save money, as obviously, it will cost more money in the long run to have to build again and also for upkeep when they are not built well. We used to have to avoid the buckets that were collecting leaking rainwater as we walked down the corridor in our high school.

Next, I seem to be talking about Facebook, society etc. We see it, political correctness, fear. We should all be allowed to be **who** we are. Respect **all**. I understand the horror of words, pictures and feeling, it is great, and very important to change that, treat people and things with respect, love and care, no matter who or what. As you would wish to be treated yourself, in an ideal world. If we all learn to love and respect our selves, then we can, in turn, love and respect everything and everyone.

For once, I thought that I would go back to sleep instead of waking at my natural, 7.45 am. I didn't, as I had all this to write. I had just put my head on the pillow at 8.25 (!!) and the phone rang. "This is a call from the Fiscal Visa Department"! People say that they have to sleep in the day. I like to get up in the day or I would have even more trouble sleeping in the night. I spent an hour trying to sleep and then used up another hour, and I had still not had a sleep. I have all the ordinary things still to do in life, all by me. Washing, eating, cooking, cleaning etc and still find time to do my own things. My walks take much longer. It took an hour to get from the end of Laggan Hill Walk to home last week. I have to go to the bottle bank, do the bins, shopping. Monday is my next "yuck", I have scans to get so it is maybe only one more Monday before I start the weekly "regeneration".

Dad wants me to help with his report. I love doing that and helping him. He is also doing so much for me in my life just now. I tried to say that I couldn't really do extra things just now, and he said that he knows, that is why he thought Monday would be good. So, he realised that I had no time for helping him. But hadn't understood what I was trying to say about mine. All this stress, time and thought is making my head worse. It is my autism but also the "save" and tunnel etc incidents when my head is going really strange.

I had a bad bleeding nose. It lasted about 25 minutes. It is still only in one nostril though.

November 2023

3rd November 2023: I am feeling a bit yucky. Doing okay. They used my left arm again today for the cannula. I am a bit bruised. I possibly have a line up my arm from giving blood on Tuesday. They say, in the info about things, to look out for lines.

I am back to having the really loud, roaring noise coming from my nose and waking me up when I lie down, since I had my bleeding nose. I have not had a blocked nose for all the time that I have been having my chemo. That is really strange as I have always had a blocked nose in the night, for as long as I can remember.

I was nearly sick in the night and feeling really ill. I had to sleep raised up on the floor cushion, a lot. I had to get up about 3.30am to take an anti-sick pill.

4th November 2023: I walked, very slowly, up to Dad's and had to lie on the couch at first. I had soup and crisps for lunch. I couldn't eat much tea.

6th November 2023: In the night I heard the owl's call.

While sitting reading in bed, I thought I saw something moving to the right, on the floor. I looked for a daddy long legs or spider (maybe, twice). I possibly did this earlier and through the flat once too but can't remember. Then 2 or 3 times in bed, on the left side and then twice across the downy. I thought it must be a spider but couldn't see anything. I flapped the downy over the floor, but nothing. It just happened in the air, twice, as I was writing this. Maybe it is the 'visual migraines' again?

It is now **12.25pm**, I didn't want to write this, as I have to be up for work tomorrow, but I just had a thought that I had had exactly the same thought before. Exactly, the same timing. As I lay there thinking about it, I knew that I have to write it. I thought it must be the same and then the next day it was, when I think that my time is going strange and with the "save" head when I met Babs. But as I thought that I should get up and write this as it was something repeated, then I couldn't think what it actually was anymore! All I know is that it was at a certain time with a quarter past then something would happen, and perhaps exactly half an hour would pass then that was bad, as it meant something else would happen, exactly like this, but now as I think and write, this is happening? I can't tell anyone this. (I know this sounds confusing and is all muddled, but I think that is important to write as it shows how my head was acting.)

In "real life", it is Monday night. I heard on Sunday, in Facebook, that Mary from work died on Saturday. It is so sad. She was such a lovely person. She left her two grown up boys, who are autistic. We were not close, personally in life but it is very thought provoking and strange when someone you know well, is just not there anymore. I better go to sleep now. Or I won't be able to switch off. Maybe I will be okay as have written this all out. Duncan has had the black mark on his face removed. It seems fine, he, hopefully, will get the stitches out on Friday.

1.06 am I am writing this in the notebook, as I can't get the paper at the foot of the bed. I have got a really hot head.

I thought that this is what happened before, so I better write it down, but haven't worked out what it is, now I am writing again. I don't know. It is all, so obviously, just a half-asleep head thing, and not real. But I am maybe just so tired as writing at the moment. Now I must go to sleep.

2.02 am I have dropped the third pen; I got the blue notebook instead of the green. I have been thinking and planning my book, all this time. I want to write the chapter headings, so at least this is not all lost:

AI computers, Data Protection, GP, Doctors, Medicine, Records, Vinyl, Shops, More and more. (These were what the chapters were, that I was planning for this book while I should have been sleeping.)

But now I must stop. My health, with the regeneration and pills together, it is just too much. In my own head, it has caused a traffic jam, my thoughts are all coming out really fast, but time, in real life, is getting in the way. I have so much more to write. (I have then made a big list of all the things that I want to talk about and that I must have been thinking about, in my head: Andrew, Alan, first year, drugs, alcohol, deaths. People we have had in the neighbouring flats good people when you get to know them. Mental Health. Dead now. Some terrified of help, drugs (GP doctors), different ways. Politically correct. Aspergers, Data Protection. Perth College, computers, technology, books, health, library.

Reading this list, I think that some of what I was wanting to say was about how Babs' brother, Andrew, used to sometimes get mistaken for a boy called Alan, that we were at school with, they looked, slightly like each other. Alan lived in the flat below me for a while. He died a few years ago. He was a lovely person but got himself into a lot of trouble, was in prison at times and had trouble with alcohol and drugs.

I have a school class photo from first year, in high school, and I used to think about how so many things had happened to the people in that photo, over the years, drugs, alcohol, deaths, suicides, losing close family etc.

We have had many troubled families and people, in the flats, over the years. It is really nice here, now. But these people, although they got into big trouble with many things, fights, alcohol, drugs, etc, they were all really nice people when talking to or interreacting with them, in normal, everyday times.

(I obviously had a lot more thoughts and things to say, but that is all I can think of, that it might have been, for just now.)

5.23 am Communication is massive and so important for **all** the world and life answers. The answer is **not** to destroy and obliterate. Money is not the answer, we need to learn and know, that we are all individuals. It is a balance between nature and nurture.

The name and category of Aspergers has been removed. We have been grouped in with the whole of autism, like our category never existed. We need unconditional love; we all have good and bad. Stop, listen and think, change, help and heal. The way to do this is to learn, listen, grow, understand. **Not** to destroy and obliterate. A lot of the trouble is, I think, fear of being sued. Wise and intelligent are not the same. We need all. Change and remove a bad name, we can do that, we can grow and learn from so much that we don't know and understand. It is good to see, hear and know other ways, worlds and viewpoints, to become part of it and understand, know and grow. It started, that I noticed, with people like Luke Jackson telling us their own stories about life, autism etc. There is great power underneath this very method of communication for people with autism. Don't destroy nor get rid of that, it took decades, but it seemed to me like a very short time. I learned about autism and suddenly I had Aspergers, myself. it has **not gone away** although they have taken the word and the whole category away. We were learning about it, so much. We were a minority. That minority found its voice, its power and started to tell its own story. It turned out, that it was, or could be, a massive majority. A majority that are not known because its very character is to communicate in a different way. Renaming us, destroying us, not just our name. It does not help history. History is really important for us to learn and develop from. Don't destroy that history because it was bad – learn and grow from it.

I grew up in a society when it was considered fine and perfectly normal to smack your children. At school, punishment was whacking you with a belt. (It was a long, thick, leather thing with cut bits at the end.) I never got the belt. I was always a good girl really (mostly).

It was quite a bit into my studies for the Child and Youth Studies degree, that I still believed that a short, sharp shock, in other words a whack, was the best way to teach certain lessons about not doing bad or dangerous things. That was what we learned and how we grew up. I then suddenly, began to understand that communication was the answer to most things in life.

Don't teach that violence is the answer. Do teach that stopping, thinking and taking time to discuss or work things out is the way to do things.

5.50 am Do not attack, fight, remove, destroy cancer. It is not a battle. It exists, there is a reason, we are All. All is a part of everyone. One and everything. Don't destroy, remove, kill, do listen, grow, learn, understand and use this to change. See, learn and develop. Fear, hate and terror need love, care, wisdom and knowledge of all different ways. To work together to grow and develop and learn. The prison system, mental health, mass trained wars, genocide, learn from it all. Listen about the concentration camps, people go there. I can't go, can't feel, can't watch news. I need to learn but feel too much.

7th November 2023: I'm in bed, reading, I'm seeing something flying past again. This time it seems bigger, perhaps a butterfly. It is small, bat size, black, fast in front of me to the right. I wonder if it's a visual migraine again or that I am just too tired?

8th November 2023: I was feeling yucky this afternoon. I was working. I did not have any appetite. I got something for lunch but didn't eat it all. I had bad diarrhoea in the afternoon. By 4pm, I was feeling headachy, tired etc. I have had a wee lie down and am feeling a bit better now at 4.30pm.

I am trying to find something to do that is not involving the computer. I am not used to having to do that. Sitting up or using the computer is making me feel yucky. Oh, what a strange wee new world this is. I am walking around in a circle. It is only 20 minutes until it is time to make tea, what can I do?

12.35am Is chemo just working away on the rest of the body, now that the lump is smaller? It is still there, does that mean it has stopped growing but is still there? If the chemo only works on the fast-growing cells. What about the rest of it?

(I've written more here. I am obviously wondering about if it will come back and balancing up whether killing more of me would be worth the shorter life balance or something like that, but I can't make any sense of what I have written.)

5.20 am (I am awake and writing, I think, about all the things that I am thinking about, everything. Spending time with Dolores, my autism times being weird as my safety net, walking, needing to do the cleaning, hairs still on the carpet from when there were so many of them falling out, meeting friends, Dad, family, not allowed to get bugs. My thumbs are going, I can't sleep for hours, it is like a time warp.)

10th November 2023: I have had a wonderful day with Dolores who really helped me, I got **all** my cleaning done. That is a massive thing to get all out of the way.

I was getting the "save" (see 24th October 2023) thing in my head, a number of times, throughout the day, both at the COOP (local supermarket) and in the flat. I thought that it must be a dealing with and speaking to people thing, but it was very interesting as I just got it just now, when typing to Dolores on the computer, when writing these notes down and when just sitting down to have my tea and throughout watching the news on tv.

If I had gone to the doctors back in May, then maybe the lump would have been less than 2cm and, maybe, I wouldn't have had to have any "Regeneration"?

(Please note that I am calling my chemo, Dr Who Regeneration now, as I can't think or talk about the word chemo without it making me feel really ill. I have started writing regeneration, as a short cut for this. I think this is also an autism, exaggerated feeling, we can have very strong, extreme feelings about things. Also note I am talking about what we used to call Aspergers here, rather than autism, as a whole, but am not to use that name anymore. I find that difficult as I feel that there is a large difference.)

13th November 2023: In the night (this morning). I have been very interested in this "save" head mode. I think it is very exaggerated autism and the Regeneration, together.

16th November 2023: I am feeling brilliant today. My left forearm was sore later, 10pm. It seems to be a wide area going from my wrist up to my elbow, of red, like sunburn.

In the night, I woke up to a clear image of my brain split into two halves, with a castellated, jigsaw type joining to the two halves. They were moving sideways towards and away from each other. That is the first time that I have had that one.

17th November 2023: I have had no sleep. I have been thinking about when I give up work. I had a great online talk, with Diane today about it all and that really helped. I then, later, had a meeting with my boss. He really listened to me, and I was able to say all the thoughts that I had about our team, my job and many things. It really helped me. It is a thought to know that I will be away from work for 6 months or more, how things will carry on, not being there to have my input etc. I trust Diane completely to carry on without me, she will be fine. I know that I just have to look after myself and get well.

18th November 2023: (A spiritual person, I "talk" in my head to what you might call spirits, my loved ones and also other beings (who I call Ones). Don't worry I am not daft, well I am (!!) but not in the way that you might think, from that. It is just my way, and I know that it is not a thing to talk about or tell people in general conversation. However, this book is far from general conversation.)

I was walking down Dollerie Terrace, asking the Ones (in my head) why unconditional love is so important. They told me that it is our way, to get lost in, to become one with All. A car then drove up and stopped, to let other cars past, and on its numberplate was ALL! That was so magical for me. The best synchronicity that I have ever had. Thank you. ♥

22nd November 2023: I want to know why I fixate on one thing for an hour or more, over and over.

23rd November 2023: It was the first of my weekly chemo treatments, today. I have very red cheeks and forehead. It felt like there was water flowing in my nose and in the night, in my ears too. It is like the start of a bleeding nose, but it is not. I had bad burning (acid reflux) coming up all night, right the way through. I took an anti-sickness tablet and raised myself up on my big floor cushion but that didn't stop it. (Please note that I am not one, in usual times, to ever take medicine, not even for a headache.)

I don't have to give myself an injection the next day, anymore. Also, the chemicals are in clear bags and not the horrible red bags.

24th November 2023: The same in the night again, with the burning coming up, all night, a bit in the day too and burpy.

I used the anti-sickness tablets but was told that I don't need to use them. It is all so confusing.

27th November 2023: The sore, blue vein on my left forearm is really hard now. The lump seems to be longer.

29th November 2023: I was at Dundee today. The oncologist said that I was doing really well, and he couldn't believe that I was still working. I had a lovely lunch with Dad on the way home. I might have a cold. I had a very runny nose last night. I have no hairs inside my nose, so it just runs out, nonstop, with nothing to stop it!

I took my hat off, in the hospital and when sitting down in the café. Sometimes I forget that I have not got my hat on. I asked the oncologist about my hair. He says I won't lose any more, during the weekly treatment, but it won't grow back until the treatment is finished. My head has been very itchy for a couple of days like when I started to lose my hair (for a few weeks or more before that).

In my 55 years I have never had constipation! I don't think that I have it now nor need a laxative, but I couldn't tell them that I don't know! I have also had the pain or discomfort that I have had at times, under my left rib since 2011.

30th November 2023: 1.45am, I am still very tired after seeing the oncologist. My Doctor Who Regeneration is on a Thursday now. One man, in the room, was nearly sick or fainting. A lady next to me had a big panic. I had to use my left arm for drawing as they couldn't get the cannula into that one. I was very tired and trying to read but not really managing to stay awake.

I am thinking about Jimmy Savile when Findlay (my brother) and I, were on holiday in Buckie. Jimmy Saville was going past in a parade that was going to a fête. He was all dressed in a gold tracksuit with all big gold rings, neck chains and a cigar. We sat on the wall and waved at him, thinking that he was wonderful. He shouted over, "I think I'm in love."

It is so creepy to think of that now. I thought that he was brilliant and loved his big armchair with all the compartments, where he got the Jim'll Fix It "medals" from. I wrote a letter to ask to be on the show and still have the letter reply with his autograph! Thank goodness I didn't get on.

Another one was Rolf Harris. I really liked and have his art book. It is still in my shelf, but I feel guilty when I see it. Yet, I do think that good work should be remembered, not just the bad when someone has done wrong, bad or evil.

Then there is the name Aspergers. It is all history; things were done very wrong in so many ways in history but that is what we know and feel now in our present society. I don't think things should be written out, nor destroyed. They are part of our history, and we should be aware of them, learn and grow from them. But then so much was built on wrong, hate, war, atrocities etc. I suppose the only good that we could possibly find, in such things, would be, to learn from them. Also to be inspired by the stories of people who lived through and survived such things. (The cd just sang survive as I typed survived there.)

But looking at the more general life of our generation, as we were learning about things, growing up. I think that perhaps, because of my autism or, perhaps, just part of being young, I had my own experiences of things and learnt and grew from them, hopefully! I think my autism may have meant that I was taken advantage of, but also that I took advantage of others. It is different now when people have such high profiles it is devastating for us to hear about people we looked up to and trusted as doing wrong. Everything is so much more reported and available for us to see and find out about. Should I watch the Jimmy Saville film? I don't want to. I don't want his photo on my page, I have his photo from that day, in Buckie, but at the time I thought that was wonderful.

Was I very innocent? Everyone says that it was obvious, but it was not obvious to me or not at the time. Maybe that was because I was younger, maybe because of my autism or both? I was shy and quiet and yet I was also, at times, a bully and confident but it was a show and an act. I also had no idea that I was a bully.

There was a boy in the primary school playground, younger than me, my family knew his family, slightly, somehow. I had fun teasing him. I had no idea that he was terrified. I was horrible. I had no idea, until his parents, or someone, told my parents and they had a word with me. I saw him in the playground, soon after that, and saw them watching to see he was all right. I felt terrible and wanted to apologise. I honestly had had no thought or idea that I was scaring him, I was just, I thought, having fun. I called over to him and he stopped, my friend told me to leave him alone. But I had just been going to say sorry and that I had not meant to be horrible at all. I just shouted over that I was sorry, and I never saw him again after that.

I then remember, in High School, drama class. We were allowed to choose a couple of periods or lessons, of more fun things and one of them, that I chose, was drama. I was there with some others, and I saw a couple of girls coming along the corridor to join the class. But when one of the girls saw me, I could hear her saying, "I'm not going in there, when that Blanche Haddow is in there". Once again, I was stunned. I had no idea or understanding that anyone would feel like that about me.

When I was in primary school, before we moved to where I have lived for most of my life, I was a "Tomboy." I wanted to be a boy. I really did. I was fascinated when a girl I knew said that she was wearing a bra. I didn't believe her. She said she would show me. We went to the toilet cubicles, and I stood up on the toilet and looked over to her cubicle, she showed me that she had a bra on! My foot then slipped and it fell int to the toilet and got soaked. That was pure curiosity on my behalf but that is the strange kind of thing that we all did as we were growing up, to find out about life. I am sure that you could, all, tell some strange stories, along similar veins, if you wanted to.

It is all part of nature and society. We were very, lucky, in our time, before that, it was all much worse, they were not told about anything at all. I was told about my periods, by my step mum, once, and given a pack of period pads which I kept in my drawer for many years, even through a house move, until the day that I needed them. After that, it was up to me to sort that sort of thing out. My Dad once asked if I wanted the book that my brothers had had in their room which told the basics of sex, but I just replied that I knew all that, already. As far as I can remember, I had read it, that book, a long time before. I can remember being on holiday with my brother, we were being looked after by some family friends. We saw some cattle mating and I shouted out, "oh look they are having piggy backs." I was very embarrassed when my brother said, "what do you think they are doing" and I worked it out. But we all learnt and found out these things, in different ways. The boys at school had "naughty" magazines, or pages out of them.

Television was a widespread and normal part of growing up and learning. During a big part of our childhood there were only three channels, Channel 4 arrived a bit later. Our tv, was black and white and only two of the channels worked. My big brothers used to get me to stand and hold the big, long television aerial! Later we got a colour tv. Televisions were much deeper and chunkier then but with much, smaller screens. I really do not like the big wall screens that people have now. I find the colours and movement far too distracting, even through windows as I am just walking along a street.

Things are so different now with the internet and social media you really could learn, see and find out about all, everything, good and bad. Miss Hyndman was our guidance teacher. I remember her telling us about periods and giving us advice about things. I learnt, a lot, from friends. I was good friends with my next-door neighbour, Tammy, for a year or so. We would play the Grease record ((vinyl), that, tapes and the radio were how we listened to music) and we were singing away, in her sitting room, to one of the songs, "Elvis, Elvis let me be, keep that pelvis far from me"". When her mum asked if we knew what that was. We were rather embarrassed when she explained! I would look at the posters on Tammy's wall and think that they were brilliant. I asked her who one man was, it was Daley Thomson, a famous decathlon star of the time. That started my obsession with him and got me watching the Olympics, for a few years.

Tammy became friends with another girl in our year, Cindy. We were all getting taken to a disco in the car, by my dad. Cindy was singing, "come up the Knock (a local hill) and I'll show you, my knee!" We were going to a disco in a tiny place called Monzie (pronounced Mon-ee). But Dad told me it was very rude. I was embarrassed by him, but I did realise that it probably was.

After that I started being best friends with, my still best friend, Babs. We had many crushes and obsessions on various boys and men! It was all so much easier then. Now I can't imagine how difficult it must be if you say or do something wrong, daft, rude etc, then it will be plastered all over social media or be recorded on phones and shared. We were so mortified by some things but at least it was only spread about by word of mouth, nothing like today.

Hopefully, it is still, all just a natural part of growing up, learning the difference between lust and love and why it matters. Hopefully, that can happen, before people are too addicted to such, easy to get and see "rude", "nasty" and much worse things. It must be so much more difficult now. There is always going to be good and bad extremes, that is part of life. We have to learn and be taught, right and wrong perhaps, but I would think that it is much more important now, to be taught how to think and judge for yourself. But the more the need for knowing and learning about such things, then perhaps the more balanced and mature, that could make some people. So, maybe, that means that social media can be a very good way to learn and develop too.

I have been very close to trouble, on a number of occasions in life. Again, I don't think that was just because of autism but all a part of life and growing up, while also being quite a different kind of person. I have sometimes fancied people who have seemed really nice, but turned out, later to be bad. A boy who I was talking to in the local town square, one day, that I fancied at school, turned out to have sexually abused someone. A man I talked to, at the job club, was in the papers for being arrested as a stalker. A boy who chatted me up, on a few occasions, was arrested for interfering with children. I think I was partly saved by my autism as I was different, didn't know the "right" ways to act or it meant people were not interested in me. I was also not in big groups etc.

I have been very lucky to have met good men in my life that could be trusted but I have also always been very tough and careful. Having brothers may have had its annoying, when young, sides at times, but it was also very good. I learnt to be careful and how to look after myself.

It is sad that I have had no partner in my life, no children or grandchildren but it has also meant that I have learnt so much more about myself. I have had the time and space to grow, become wiser and very spiritual. That has been my coping mechanism. It is good for old age and being alone, to have trust and faith. I know of many ladies who are on their own now but they, mostly all, have children or grandchildren, that has been, I think, their saving grace.

2.38 am (Oh, my goodness, all these thoughts were just in one night! It must have been a very wide-awake night.)

I am searching for my pen, but it is right there in front of me. My tummy is getting a bit crushed, with me sitting up, but the burning is not too bad, I got pills this time.

Ai can give answers to what management should do, work our supermarket tills and do our DTP (Desk Top Publishing) jobs but that is forgetting what we need and that is people, caring and personal service, **not falseness**. That might be our saving grace. We, society, think that Ai will mean losing many jobs. Maybe" higher level" people think that it is us that will lose the jobs. Actually, it could be the false, high up, or impersonal jobs that could be done and answers found so much easier by Ai. It might be what saves our society. We might find that what we need is real, caring, thoughtful, empathetic workers to help us. That is what is missing from a cold machine. That is what we need. **Communication** is the answer to **all.**

Our incredible NHS (National Health Service) is too busy to take time to listen to individuals to interconnect departments (education, social work etc). Communication could save massive amounts of inconvenience but, much more importantly, that could enable us to learn, evolve and develop so much more and also, save us a fortune.

The wealth of our college is in its wisdom, not its money. Ai could learn that, teach us or we could learn that and teach ourselves to solve so much.

(Ah I see now. This must have been me planning what I wanted to say for my video that I made about the college, us losing our jobs and what they could do to sort their situation.)

3.16 am I am having to sit, right up to avoid my tummy crunching. My thumbs and fingers are going, going, going. (This was me not being able to switch off and my thumbs are, I think, autistic stimming which I discuss some more in my Video Diaries on my *See Salt Tears* Website.) I am wondering if I should keep going with them (my thumbs) or if it might be better to try and stop them. If that would help? No, it means that I won't get to sleep. The steroids and stress are stopping me. The oncologist said I was obviously very anxious. I wonder how he knows. It must be my body language as I have not said anything. I want to ask about the over working enzyme that they mentioned when I had to go into the hospital for my fluttery heart. But I better not bother him. He shook my hand. I gave him my hand and realised how much I don't look at people.

During my Dr Who Regeneration, it is great, as I can look at my drawing while I am talking to the nurse. I don't have to look them in the eyes. I didn't know that I do that.

Letitia, who was looking after me in the chemo room, said, "you've done it, 10 minutes up." I looked at the treatment bag and said, "what?". She replied, "10 minutes are up, while I wait". (They have to stay with you for 10 minutes to make sure that the treatment is going in properly and that there is no bad reaction.) Maybe she thinks that I don't like the time when they wait with me, as I don't talk but I've talked more than ever today. About my mum, Christmas, playing Cranium, Christmas stockings etc. I even asked about her holidays.

I don't think that trying to stop my thumbs or waiting and not writing things down in the night, would help, just now. It would just get me more hyper, more awake. Perhaps it would help calm me, but I think that it helps me to get in the right mind to get my thoughts out.

When I can't sleep, it is actually the opposite to the Duracell battery bunny. (For those of you who don't know or are too young to know the Duracell battery bunny advert. It was a toy bunny that drummed at high speed when it had a Duracell battery put in it.) It is the steroids, I think. No, not opposite, the same. Perhaps my thumb rubbing is me trying to get my body to work at the same speed as my mind, emotionally, as I have more time when I am relaxed at night without having to deal with work, people, stress etc. I think this is when stopping work is really going to help. I feel bad but it is a very good idea and sensible.

Yes, I think that rubbing my thumb and forefinger together is my subconscious way to change my vibration and speed me up. That is very interesting and important, I think. It is now **3.29am**!

It is great now, it being Thursday, for my Regeneration, as that leaves Friday to myself. I don't have to think about getting up. I wanted to change it to a Friday as that is what I was used to and fitted in with my work, but now I am glad, it is good that way.

I am still awake at **7.45am**.

December 2023

4th December 2023: Last Thursday, it was just too much for me in the treatment room. It was crowded, there was a flickering light outside that kept catching my eye, the staff trolleys were right beside me, a man was very ill, the nurses were talking, the lady patients were chatting, beepers on the machines going off etc. I was awake, after that, until 7.45am. I want to tell them.

I told the lady, on the phone today, during my checkup call. But I said it would be the steroids. I feel as if my autism doesn't matter as it is such an important, busy place. But it doesn't go away. This is all very stressful. I have been thinking about my life, it is very stressful. It feels like everyone forgets about my autism and I don't suppose it is important, as I have done fine without knowing that I had it, for 51 years. But it is important. The pain is in the left of my tummy today, as well as my left side. I don't have anyone to talk to about this. It just feels like it is very important. It just feels like it is not important. The stress of the room really shows me, how it, my autism, is, **really important**.

The advert on television says that one in two people will have cancer. I never wanted to hear or listen to that before. At least, I knew, for sure, that it wouldn't be me. I was wrong!

In some of the many words that they give you to read with advice, there is one thing, out of it all, that I really like and that is, that your food is your medicine. I really like that; it is great advice.

My "baldy heed" is like the wee hole in the cooking pot lid. The steam comes out when I am in bed, and it is very handy!

11th December 2023: Why does my tummy not work? Why does the food just pile up and not come out?

There is no one to talk to. Everyone is so lovely and say that they will help in any way with lifts etc. No one really has anyone to talk to. Everything is about time and money. Even people with partners, I don't think that they really do have someone to talk to. I sometimes wonder if same sex couples are able to communicate more but that is far too general although a very interesting thought, when thinking about the type of problems that are discussed in Men are from Mars, Women are from Venus, type things.

I have a blocked nose; I need fresh air. Sue has Covid. It is all very confusing. I think that my hot flushes might be back. I always opened the window to help when I couldn't get to sleep, now I am too scared to, in case I get a cold, chill, ill, as I am not able to fight things off (the treatment kills off the white blood cells). I have opened It.

4.13 am I am grumpy as I can't sleep. I need to think, it is the steroids and maybe the menopause. When the doctor phoned, she asked about my mental health, but I can't think or say things quickly on the phone, or in any conversation. I want to write a letter. Actually, writing this is very therapeutic. Maybe I don't need sleep. I do have someone to talk to, I have myself. This is incredible. It is not the way any of us, in society, do it. I wonder why not? As no one is on their own but then millions of people are. They must be so lonely. Maybe the answer is, ourselves. We can really sort it, and things. This is so super and brilliant. Like my whole journey in life has worked up to this. I must watch, as I am getting cold, at the back of my neck, but it is so much fresher.

I better get snuggled back down now and watch out for my neck and a chill, close the window maybe.

12th December 2023: I gave blood today. I have decided that it is constipation. Katrina, one of the brilliant and lovely, nurses at the health centre, said it will be. I feel so daft that I don't know that. I have never had constipation in my life.

13th December 2023: I woke up at 8am (a much better sleep). I woke at 4am but got back to sleep. I woke up to a picture of my big brother, Chris, taking a Scrabble move in the shape of the "Crown of Bonnie Scotland", it was like my wee silver crown brooch.

I had a great day. In the morning, I went with Babs to visit Andrew and the graveyard. We found her great uncle's grave. I know graveyards have horrible connotations, but I also find them fascinating and very thought provoking. I love all the special old carvings and things. Then I met my good friends, Helen and Dolores for lunch, at my favourite restaurant, Delivinos.

16th December 2023: I had a great birthday meal today at dads. with my brother Findlay and his family. I ate all of it and loved it. My tummy is not working yet but I am feeling really good. I am tired and have bruised hands. They, the family, all wore hats for me, for the photos, which was really lovely of them.

17th December 2023: I have bad constipation. Sorry for this but . . . when it finally arrived, it was massive. I thought I would have to get a saw to break it up in the toilet! It took three flushes to get rid of. For two weeks I have taken the pills to stop the burning (reflux) coming up. They have worked great but really, they work, apparently, by stopping the acid which digests food. So, I think this might be causing the trouble. I don't trust them now, as I think that they will just give me more pills to stop constipation. I will ask tomorrow when they phone, to see if I can stop taking the "burn" pills and just take them when I need. But I know it was really bad. I hope they understand and listen and that it is better.

18th December 2023: I was to meet Babs when I got up, but she wasn't answering the door. She was at the loo, but I was really worried. I didn't phone in case I woke her up but left a note through the door. My autism shows through, in my love of times to do things. So, I went to the COOP. Then walked past Paul's old place. (Paul was a good school friend.)

I am stressed. My tummy was very bad yesterday, with constipation. I had a bleeding nose. The Perth lady, on the phone, said that I am allowed to cut down the "burn" pills. My tummy is not right, my ears are not right, and I am tired.

19th December 2023: I had a brilliant day out to Doune Castle with Dad and Duncan. I had to give blood in the morning. It was confusing as I wanted to get going on my day out, but Dad, Sue and Duncan, all turned up in the Health Centre Carpark with my presents and to say Happy Birthday. So, we went back to the house. I stayed calm but the slightest change to plans, or stress, sets me off, I go all shaky. (It really is like the autism is very exaggerated by all this.)

I thought that I would try taking baking soda to help with the acid reflux as I like more natural things. So, I did, for three days, but I had the most terrible diarrhoea tonight. I think that I have been really daft with that experiment. So, I can't use that now. Google is very confusing on the subject; I am very tired. I think that I am doing great. I had my sore, when bending, tummy all day, but I think it is stress. It was like the state when I was working. I need to think about Dad and Sue, but it takes so much effort for me to think. It is just the usual sort of things that make me stressed, but it seems so much higher, and my level of coping is so much lower, I just can't do it. I am doing great I just have to have trust and faith. Keep cheery and get good sleep.

23rd December 2023: Today, when walking up the street with Dad, as I said the word, "nice", in my conversation, a big sign saying "Nice", was in the shop window.

Playing Trivial Pursuit with Dad, using the two boxes that have hundreds of questions in them. We both asked a Snoopy question, one after the other.

25thDecember: We all had a great day, all went well.

When wrapping my presents, a while ago, I created and wrote out some gift tags using old Christmas cards from the year before. When going to put one of the tags on a present, I couldn't find them anywhere. I searched the whole of the flat, round about and all the bins!

Today, Sue opened up the present that I gave her. One of the things in it was a new sponge bag. She opened the sponge bag to see inside it and brought out a small bundle of things. There they were, the lost gift tags!! I know my head is in a very strange state but how on earth did they get in there?!

28h December 2023: Dr Who Regeneration today, I had very high blood pressure, apparently. I've got a very dry mouth, sicky and diarrhoea feeling tummy, after lunch, but fine and hunky dory. I know that Granny was with me in the room today, as I heard one of the patients telling the nurse about a "Helen Roberts".

29th December 2023: I am really tired, can't see very well to read.

30th December 2023: I had a lovely morning with Dad and Sue. Dad and I were doing his jigsaw. We talked to my brothers, Chris and Duncan, on the computer. My eyes are still really bad. I needed the magnifying glass to do the jigsaw.

At home, I tried to read again and nearly couldn't. I ate my tea and am doing a bit better this evening. I had a very scary and strange state of head while making my tea. I had to keep telling myself what to do and be careful, in my head, as I was going along. Time has gone wonky again (it is like the "save" experience). It is sometimes much earlier and sometimes much later than I expect.

I didn't sleep much at all. I couldn't switch off.

31st December 2023: I had a bit of a cough yesterday, but feeling well and good. Dad had a bit of one too. I have decided not to go up for the New Year meal. I had a great day and walk. I was a bit wonky this afternoon, having to tell myself what is what, in my head, but doing good. Just **very** tired.

January 2024

1st January 2024: I felt hunky dory, I slept well, so I went up to the garden to see if Dad was okay. I did a Covid test with Sue. It turns out that I have Covid! Dad and Sue do not.

Dad is really coughing but feels fine. I have come home. I hadn't seen anyone else nor was I at the COOP yesterday, which I usually always am. I can't get Oncology on the phone. I think that they will just be really, busy and short staffed. It will be like prison having to stay in. (It is the first time that I have had Covid, I have done so well and been so careful through all those years, lockdown etc.)

It is a beautiful blue sky. I have a million things to do. I just would like to hear what they say on the phone, in case they say that I am to go to Dundee.

I am feeling really daft and dopey. I went to put the bin dates on the new calendar and found out that I have made a 2023 calendar! So, mine, Diane's and my friend Ruth's calendars, that I gave them for Christmas presents, are all wrong, as it should, of course, be 2024. I can't do much as my head is wonky. I think that I am just stressed. I think I must have been doing loads wrong and that people have been lovely and so patient, and I have been thinking that I have been fine. "Daft but ga'in aboot" as Granny used to say.

Dad and Sue are so lovely. Dad has a really bad cough, and I have reverted back to just thinking about myself. So, the autism is coming out, when I can't think. Dad is in his eighties and Sue had Covid back in December. They must have been so stressed and neither of them have shown it. They, and all the family and friends have been so lovely.

I haven't coughed much at all, no cold or anything. I think my head is just stressed. My left side is sore now. It is fascinating, really. I got really stressed at not being able to get the Perth ladies on the phone. I thought that they would be there today. I phoned Dundee and they just put me through to the Perth room. Nothing to stress about. It is like, in normal times, when I believe things when I am half asleep. Sue helped when I phoned and Dad too.

It really helps me to write all this. It is like talking for hours to someone but so much easier than that. It is very therapeutic.

3rd January 2024: I am coughing more today. It is a very chesty cough but still not that much. It has been cold or rather very misty since New Year. I did a 25-minute walk, on the spot, with my hat and coat on, in the sunroom in front of the open window. The neighbours must think that I am mad! I am tired and my eyes are still bad.

It is strange, every now and then I realise that my arms, fingers, back and shoulders have no hair. It is weird not to have to pluck my chin or moustache at all I used to have to do that every night. (Yes, a lot of us ladies do have to do such things too!) I think, oh that would be great if it stays this way. Then I think, **NO**, cause that might mean that the rest won't grow back too, my hair in my nose, ears etc. Whatever is going wrong with my eyes? I am just tired, I hope, but I can hardly read, and computers can be too much. Then my head goes wonky. It is hilarious that I still have hairy legs and toes! Of all the body hair I would not want, it is the only hair that has decided to stay!

I want my lovely hair back. It will be lovely not to have to hide or think about hats. But I do love just getting out the bath and my hair is dry, no drying. My wee wooden, nail brush, that I have been using for my hair or baldy heed, is so cute and soft. I loved the wind on my head, earlier in the year, when the weather was still warm enough for that.

I have a funny tuft of hair growing back in front of my right ear. It is the most hair that I have.

The front, bottom of my mouth, gums, has been really sore for a week.

6th January 2024: I waited until late afternoon to do the Covid test. I am now negative. ☺ Lovely.

7th January 2024: I went my Sunday walk. I was worried in case the test was wrong. It was a lovely walk. I wasn't home until 2pm. I went to the COOP. I soon forgot about the Covid and got back into the swing of being out and about again. It is lovely not to have Covid.

9th January 2024: I am feeling really good. Even my mouth is getting better. Sometimes, when I just wake up maybe, I see electric white/silver lines or lightening zig zag in front of my eyes.

11th January 2024: Dr Who Regeneration today. I didn't get home until 4pm. Sue took me today, Dad still has Covid. I phoned Sue, using the mobile, to say when the second big treatment bag had been attached. She was in the waiting room by this time. It was too cold outside for her to wait in the car. I was stressed at having to use the phone. (I don't use mobile phones so am not used to doing that.) But it was fine. I put her number on the phone a couple of days ago.

(It will be difficult, I expect, for many of you to understand me not wanting to use a mobile phone, but I don't. I do have a wee black one though, which has been really, handy throughout this, when on my walks, to phone Dad to come and pick me up, so I can get a good walk but not have to walk back at the end. I get very much extra stressed just now and I don't like changes or things that I am not used to at the best of times. But for my treatment, Dad just sits in the car later in the day and waits for me to get finished so I don't need to phone him.)

This morning, I had to wait in the waiting room with two other ladies, as the treatment room was so busy. I was taken about 1 ½ hours before them and they were finished about ½ an hour before me. It is strange how we are all so different with what treatment we get.

It took so long today as they were so busy, so I was left waiting for some treatment bag changes and at the end for a while. But it was okay as I was so sleepy. It was two people's last treatment today. I heard the staff saying to ring the bell. I wonder what bell they are to ring.

At night my thumbs were going, and I couldn't switch off at all. There was too much talking and things going on in the waiting room. In the treatment room, I was sitting near a lady from the same town as me, so we were chatting, then being late and waiting for the changes of bags etc.

15th January 2024: I am feeling good this afternoon. My tummy finally worked, and I slept much better. I was really freezing in the night. I needed four blankets on top of my downy, but it was really cold. I went through the parks for my walk round.

I put my new bee stickers on my wheelie bins. (I love them, they are big bumble bees. I have put them under the handle of each bin so that I can tell that it is my bin.) Dad phoned to say he finally got negative for Covid last night. ☺

It is so lovely to have time to relax. I have been doing the crystal jigsaw that I got for Christmas. It is a beautiful sunny day, so the light is good. I can just stop when my eyes get tired.

I got fed up in the night. There are only five more Dr Who's to go, which is great, but it is all too vague now. What will happen next? I don't know exactly what happens next, nor who to ask. I don't want to ask the Dundee man (oncologist) in case I have to go there. I am having a bit of a panic.

I don't want change. I have got used to the love, care, routine, help etc. I understand why some people might, subconsciously, stay ill!

But thinking about it all, in my head, helped me calm down. I realise that I do know, roughly, what is going to happen and can just be. (My, being not doing, mantra.) If it, the cancer, comes back then that is what happens. I am reading in the *Synchronicity Key* book (David Wilcock) about primal fear. What happens if something happens? I know perfectly well that I will just deal with it. I have been thinking about my nephew and all his medication. I wish that they would work with him, maybe they do? They should never have started him on medication.

(I realise **many** people need medication and that it can really help. I was just writing down the thoughts that I was having, as I had them.)

18th January 2024: It went well today at Dr Who. I got

a seat in the corner. I couldn't see the clock, so I was a bit bothered about Dad and not knowing how long he would be waiting for me. I thought that it must be about 4.30pm but it was actually only 3.30 when I got out. The light is getting better, it stayed light until we got home about 4.05pm. Neither Dad nor Sue like driving in the dark now.

I got a bit muddled as I thought that we were on the first blue bag, but it was actually the second, when Letitia said it was only 15 minutes until the flush. (They put a bag of salt water through after treatment called a flush.)

It was much more relaxed today. There was no one much to talk to at all. It was comfy and peaceful. Really nice. I drew a chaffinch today. There were only cheese or cheese and tomato sandwiches to choose from today with brown bread. (I find the idea of cheese sandwiches so boring and although I love tomatoes, I never have them on sandwiches as I think that they will make the bread soggy.) I chose cheese and tomato; it was actually okay. It was nice cheese. I also had a box of currants that Sue gave me last week.

(See the drawings that I did, during the treatment, on the My Journey Through Cancer page on my See Salt Tears website: Drawings Gallery)

I thought that I would try with no acid reflux pills, but just after midnight, I started feeling it on my left side and feeling the burning coming up. I was burpy just before bed or sleep time. I thought that I better get up and take one, I had it ready. I read on for a while, it will just do more damage if I let the stuff burn up. I sat up to write this, to give me time for the pill to work. The steroids will maybe keep me awake anyway. I use my lovely pink salt lamp to see by when I am writing these notes.

I am cold. It has been freezing, for a number of days, but beautiful. It is to get milder and to turn to rain tomorrow.

Later, I was burpy, I have a bit of burning now. I better try cutting down rather than stopping the pills, next week. Maybe I could just take them on the treatment day, rather than all three days? I don't want constipation as it was very bad last week. I am doing good but farty too! I have had egg mayonnaise for a few days and can smell it (Sorry about this people, but it is what I have written!) So, it is moving in the right direction. I will see if that wins out?!

My mouth is a bit dry; I only took a bit of water with the tablet, so maybe I should have had the whole wee glass. But I had three glasses this evening. I don't know about the balance of dry and if it is **just** in my mouth.

My left hand is sore, and a bit raised. I wanted them to use my left hand but maybe it is not good yet. I got my right and left mixed up when I was saying which hand I wanted them to use and when thinking here about what side I was sleeping on. I think I got my words wrong when I was telling Letitia about being stressed.

12.59am, I have now put the light back on as my thumbs are going. I am getting my hot flushes again. Maybe it is better for them to get finished, if this is all hormone related, and because I had a late menopause?

I am wondering about me getting muddled with all this, there seems to be a trouble with my left and right. I think people on the autistic spectrum maybe do a lot more work with that, than people realise. I think that I say, "left", in my head, then picture and feel (again in my head) my left hand and then say left. Perhaps I just can't do all that extra processing work just now. I said the wrong word to Dad in the car. It was the opposite to what I should have said. I can't remember what the word was now.

At the treatment, my seat was in the corner, I was facing

the window so a different way round than usual. Which would make me more muddled about left and right.

I wonder what the word I got wrong in the car was.

Last week, in the waiting room, when the other patient asked me what type of breast cancer it was, I was trying to say right side, but I didn't know. Each time people ask, or I tell, I point to my right boob but twice now I can't think what side to point to. The lady had meant type like, triple negative, so I got that wrong too, but I find it interesting that I couldn't do my left or right. I can't think.

2.55am

It is snowing outside. I was remembering, when learning to drive, being told about the lady who wrote Left and Right on the correct hands, for her driving test. Also, about how many people in our family are controlling or rather, like to be in control. It is a way to cope with the autistic spectrum. But also, the generations before, passed these things down. A mixture of both nurture and nature.

Me (female), I am the same, but I've also got my own territory and hide away. When Tom used to own and live in my flat, then Dad would come to visit him. I hated when Dad would arrive and move my armchair for their game of Scrabble. He would shout hello and bang loudly on the metal door knocker. I got a row one time for not hearing him when he was picking me up, but he was early. I understand all these things and none of them mattered but they all mattered to me, as it was my territory, and that is where I am in control, to keep myself safe and happy. That was all a long time ago. Now I pretty much live in peace and have my own territory, to myself.

Now I can get sympathy and understanding. But Dad, etc, never thought or chose to find out whether they were on the autistic spectrum, so they don't get any sympathy for similar traits.

I was awake from 12.00 to 7.30am, very stressed and upset about the changes and end of Dr Who Regeneration, the vagueness and the Dundee appointments. I am too tired to think. Dad is going to my aunty and uncles. He needs and deserves a holiday. Sue is taking me to Dundee on Monday 22nd. Dad is taking me on Thursday morning to Dr Who Regeneration. I didn't know what to do about Monday 29th. Then I had every thought in the world! It is these steroids, and I should have taken an acid reflux pill. I had to get up at 12.10am and put the light on.

19th January 2024: I got up and am feeling much better. I am very tired. I have noticed lines across my nails. They are interesting white bands like the bad years in tree rings! It has been very cold, so I think that is why my hands are getting wee cuts. My hand was very bruised and swollen from the treatment yesterday.

22nd January 2024: I am extremely stressed; my tummy is very tight, and I am very burpy. It is a strange mixture as I am doing really good and had a great long sleep through last night, even although there was a big storm and the wheelie bins were flying about the street. Also, my tummy worked today, so that is brilliant. But I had the ultrasound scan in Dundee today at 3.20pm.

Sue took me, she was worried and stressed, as she can't see so well now in bad weather and when it gets darker, as the appointment was later in the day. It turned out that it only took a wee while and we were home by 5.05pm. It was dark by then, but we did fine.

At the hospital, I asked Sue the time, it was 3.15pm. I was meant to be in the room for my appointment for 3.20pm. I had to run but I can't run now. I tried. My legs were all wobbly. I got to the place that I was meant to be, said sorry that I was late, and the lady said that I wasn't! It was only 3.20.

I couldn't think. I lost my big yellow hanky when waiting for Sue to manage to park the car (it can be really difficult and take a long time to find a space). It turned out, in the hospital, that my hankie was in my pocket all along. But I need my big hankies, so I got very stressed. They are like my cuddly as Dad always had them as I was growing up. I am writing this so fast that my tummy is tight, but it is good to get it written. I can't deal with people. It is lovely that they care but I can only think and look after myself I just can't deal with them.

I thought that I was to get the seed marker thing put in today, for my operation. I was dreading it, as I am not healing so well, also you are not allowed a bath after it and my baths are my therapy. But it was just a jelly scan (ultrasound) and really quick. I said, "have you not got to do the bit under my arm" and he replied that he had already done that. I am in a right muddle. Everything is just so vague. I would do fine if it was all in Crieff and there was no travelling, getting lifts etc.

When I get there, everyone is so lovely. The storm is getting really wild again. I had to lift all the rubbish and wheelie bins up around the garden today and it has been a bit too much for me. It is really strange what I don't know that I can't do now. I reckon it would really help to have someone to talk to (a professional) any time but that I didn't have to go to them, just be able to type to them. I never want to say something is wrong, in case I have to go through to Perth or Dundee.

(Synchronicity there, I typed "I don't know", as the CD sang "when I don't know what I am doing"!)

It is all so interesting and fascinating. My head and I are doing so well and great, but I also get so muddled and tired.

I hope that my book will help others find some answers, in a similar situation. It must be so difficult doing all this with a partner or family. There would be good and bad things to that.

I have wee cuts on my fingers that are not healing well.

I worry all about things, many that just don't happen. I was so worried about getting the seed marker, but I wasn't getting that yet anyway. I just need peace and quiet, time and calm to help me to relax and look after myself. But I also rely on others but can't cope with them at the same time, if I have to deal with them.

I am just so tired. I can't switch off when dealing with or after dealing with people. Family and friends are so important, there is nothing more so when you realise that you might die. But I just need peace and quiet, time to myself.

The storm had blown the roof bit off the hospital entrance, so I had to go round another way, which made me panic even more.

On Saturday, I had a lovely time at Dad's, playing our board game, but I sometimes have to help Dad with the game. I love that, usually. I am so patient and calm but now I just get grumpy. It is still brilliant but then I can't sleep or switch off. It is all very fascinating.

With my friends, I want to meet them but then I can't sleep as I know that I have to get up in the morning even although I don't have to get up in the morning anymore. It is just a thought having to think and remember to do things. It doesn't work. I can't sleep for thinking I must do that. It was a great idea to stop work.

I am getting all burpy, and burning is coming up. I can't believe how much stress affects me. The burps and discomfort in my left side, all that time, since 2011, maybe it was all just from stress? I am hearing neighbours, I wonder if they can hear my very loud, nonstop burps? They must think that it is horrible. I just hear their switches or plugs or whatever it is. When stressed, like this, I am so tired, and my eyes can't see so well.

Oh, I have more and more to say and write. It is definitely going to be one of those nights. I am worried that people reading this book will just think that I am moaning, fussing etc about nothing and so, not like the book. But this is not nothing, it most definitely is something. I reckon it could really help others and that I have to do this and be brave. Write it, write it all.

I have to forget about what people might think and that they might not like the book or think that I am just being stupid, moany, silly etc. That they might think that there is nothing whatsoever to go on about. But this is so much. The autism is so real and if I even helped one more person with this, or in a similar situation, then that would be like someone helping me right now and that would be wonderful. So, I am going to be brave and just do this, for me, and hope that it helps someone and others too.

I had a twitchy eye on Saturday and now, again, today, I think it is stress. I have calmed down now, with reading. I have got that all out of my system now. I now feel dirty or bad, like in the old days when I was out on a night out, and talked or completely got taken up in the crowd, drunk, a party, or talking, or fun and let all my defences down. It is a weird thing, like I am ashamed and done something wrong.

My thumb is throbbing with wee cuts that won't heal up quickly.

See Salt Tears

There was a writing competition that I entered through work, and I found out today that I won it. Brilliant. ☺

It was a challenge to write a story in 150 words and to include the word December or Christmas. Here is what I wrote:

Christmas Creative Writing Competition

Always Here

Flower colours are bright, the sun is out, a butterfly flutters about. The stunning blue of the damselflies catch my eyes as they go about their busy lives.

The river carries on its never-ending flow and splash towards the sea. I smell the earth, the freshness, the greenery.

Sunshine sparkles on the water. I love those sparkles, the magic. They make me think of fireworks. While I watch and listen to the fireworks, I see the glitter that conjures up the magic of Christmas.

Festive times, the advent calendar opens its doors one by one, angels and presents. The trees, the smells.

A loud splash, the electric blue and orange of a kingfisher as it sprays water around diving in for its next meal. I'm brought back to earth.

It's tangerine time. My thumb presses into the skin and the refreshing, uplifting orange scent, bursts out at me.

25th January 2024: 2.26 am, it was like the hare and tortoise race, when I was trying to get myself to the scan appointment in Dundee. I was puffing and struggling but the tortoise won in the end! The reception lady said, "you are not late". I asked the time, and it was 20 past, the time that my appointment was. I am just so used to us Haddow's, we are always 5 or 10 minutes early. I was out really quickly. Sue had barely started reading her book. We were well on our way back to Crieff before dark. It was dark here around 3.30pm a month ago but now about 4.45. My friend Liz always said it got lighter again by Valentines Day, when we used to get the bus to work.

Today Dad took me, and Sue got me back, from my treatment. Last week I was very stressed, I couldn't tell if we were on the first or the second treatment bag. This week, with help from Letitia, I did better. I was able to phone Sue using my wee black mobile. Sue was saying that she knows I don't like mobiles but that it had been so handy for me lately, and she is right. It has enabled me to go on my walks, which has been so therapeutic.

I am awake from my Dr Who Regeneration. Maybe it is from the steroids? I had questions to ask, last Thursday, but they are so busy. I got to ask them today. I asked about having been given steroids for the last 6 months if it would be a problem to just stop. She just looked at me and said that it was a very small amount, and they were not stopped slowly or anything. But I don't think that they have any idea that I really, never take any medicine whatsoever. I can never believe when the ladies at work etc all take paracetamol and nowadays Ibuprofen etc. I also think that the steroids really affect me, much more, with my autism. But, as with many of the other things, I have also heard many of the other patients not liking them and the nurses telling them it is a false high. But then I have also found out that we are all getting very different treatment. The other ladies, that I have got to know, are always finished before me.

I can see my neck and shoulders looking muscly and I am not sleeping when taking them. But that is also definitely from stress, change, autism and dealing with people.

I got Tracy when giving blood. I tried to say how stressed I was about going to Dundee etc. She asked, "do you not have someone looking after you?". I said yes, but if someone is looking after you, then you have to look after them. She laughed and said, "us ladies are terrible at the best of times never mind with what you are going through".

My eyes are gritty and tired.

2.44am: I got up for water before this. I have to sit up because of my throat, I can feel the Dr Who acid reflux. I took them, the reflux pills, before bed this time.

3.17 am: I am thinking about the history of technology, home computers. When I started working with computers, there was no mouse, menus etc. Now everyone uses phones and older people, especially ladies, that I know, seem to use iPads. I can't see some things on the laptop screen never mind a much smaller screen. On the bus I see the people all flicking through things so quickly on their phones, they hardly seem to spend any time on anything, just fly through it all. I was saying more here, about a website that I found, created by an autistic man who loves Lego. But I can't read my writing.

28th January 2024:

(See Video Diaries on See Salt Tears Website 28th January 2024)

29th January 2024: I have my big MRI (Magnetic Resonance Imaging) scan this morning, in Dundee, at 11am, it was meant to be 8.30am! It is just now, 5.51am. I have had a blocked-up nose for the last couple of hours, it is like an allergy or maybe too much central heating. I haven't done the cleaning.

(The things I am talking about here may be very uncomfortable for people, however I am still going to write them as they are very important and all part of the journey that I went through.)

I want to ask about why I have cancer and what happens if it comes back. Why it grew so fast. If it is a very aggressive form, then why does it not just come back? The chemo has worked or is working, which is brilliant. Perhaps it has even helped with other things, but how can I do that over and over? It is ruining my heart, body, ears, eyes, head, tummy, taste etc, etc. I used to have such a sore back. I haven't had that in all this time. Has it sorted it? Babs and Andrew both had really sore backs but a different kind, I think. Is my lower left rib discomfort to do with when I had my monster cyst? And more. I want to ask the oncologist about all these things, but I don't want to have to go to Dundee. So, I don't. I have no one else to ask.

Babs had no one to talk to about her own thoughts and feelings. The staff are all brilliant, amazing and wonderful but have their own jobs and areas of expertise. They don't have time for questions or talking. That is a massive part missing. They have an amazing amount of knowledge, experience and understanding. It would be great if they were given time to deal more with questions and helping us to understand.

I am scared, in the night, that it will just come back. But I know that if I die or remembered that if I die, then that is my journey. I just have to enjoy myself and get on with it.

I have been sad thinking, when I saw the red squirrel yesterday, about Mary (from work, who died), she loved squirrels, but I shouldn't be sad. I should be happy and think of her nicely. Why are we sad? Andrew, Mary, mum etc. We all have very short lives. A hundred years, a thousand years, time flies. We have to just get on with it and enjoy the journey.

I have been scared a couple of times. I gave BB, the cuddly dog that my brother gave me, a cuddle and had a cry. I miss having a partner for love but that has two sides. Thank goodness I don't have one, in many ways. I just get on and don't think about it. There is good and bad to that, but it really helps. That is why I don't want to think about nor talk about my Dr Who Regeneration, as doing that makes me feel sick. Ill, like when you have eaten something bad and got really sick from it, then you can't eat or think about that food again.

But, underneath, maybe I am just in denial. It is my way of coping by not thinking about it or dealing with it. Maybe that is a good thing, maybe it is not, but it is what I do.

If I die, I die. I know that I am going to live until I am over 100, I have always known that. That knowledge is what got me through when I had my monster cyst, in 2011. But what if I don't? Then that is just my journey. I know that I will then be with my mum, Granny etc. I know (I know we all have different beliefs, but these are mine) that "life" goes on, just not the physical body. But it is the sudden, just not being there, of Mary and Andrew. It just doesn't make any sense. They are there and then, suddenly, not there. It is so weird. I don't know if I can or should rather write all this part of my book. It will be horrible for friends and family. It is funny how people love and want to read or watch about wars, death, horror etc but not actually think about our real life and death. Perhaps it is all a safety net, like the old horrible fairy stories, nursery rhymes etc that we don't get or have anymore. Folk lore.

My old boss said that my book made her laugh and cry. I

can't do this to my family and friends. But actually, I can. It is really important for me, us, society to think about it, death. It is fear and a complete unknown, but yet every single one of us deals with it, all our lives and we all die. Born and die, the two things that we all have in common. We just want it to be a long time away. So, we don't talk about it, read, watch or discuss it. It is just not a thing that we need to bring to the surface.

With my autism, I think, that I want to think about things, sort them out, discover, find out why, how, what for. It is a good, new thing to focus on and wonder about. It is not bad, not negative, not giving up. It is annoying when everyone says you must fight. It is not a battle, not a war. It is just life, just a journey. Have it, love it. Love it. Peace. Peace, love, happiness, fun, laughs. This really helps. I have plenty of time, days and nights to sleep. This writing, talking it out, thinking, is brilliant, so therapeutic etc. Just write it, love it, get it all out of my system.

I have a bad mouth and gums, the lower middle. I have a taste like tablets, sick feeling in my tummy. The alarm is to go at 8am it is now 6.21.

With Mary, Andrew etc, it is so much harder with their family and kids, Mary's boys. She must have been so scared and yet maybe not. Some people, just them, knew, they are wise and intelligent, they know what it is and what will be. They just do it and get on with the journey. It is really weird to think about. They must have known just not talked about it or, not to many. Write it in a book? It is weird how it is not nice for my family and friends but very good for someone, anyone, someone somewhere to read. For great fear or terror, let's talk, think, wonder, discover and deal with it, face it. It is life and death.

8.33am: I am up and getting ready. I am worried that the lump is still there when there is only 3 weeks of chemo to go.

In Dundee, they had trouble getting the cannula into me. My arm is all bruised. The scan machine was fine. I actually really love it! It is sad as my ears seem to be much worse than they were, 6 months ago. I could hardly hear what Alexander Armstrong was saying this time on the Classical radio. (They give you headphones to wear and play music through them, for you. I chose classical to relax me.)

My left arm is still sore. They tried the right arm, three times. Then whacked my hand to get it to work better. I said, "em, mind that my arm is sore", she was so sorry but, luckily, we both saw the funny side of it! It is still yellow now because the treatment makes me heal very slowly.

Graham (Babs' husband) very nicely took me. We had lunch at a great farm food café on the way home. It was great but too much for me, with all the talking. I just can't talk about bad things etc. It was too long a day, and I was very tired.

My mouth has that tablet kind of taste again. My tummy worked this morning, but I have been uncomfortable on the left side all day. I am in a bit of a strange sate. It is just too much stress, like when I was at work. I have a twitchy left eye now.

30th January 2024: I had to phone the doctors for a new sick note as it runs out 5th February.

My only body hair left now is mostly just lower legs and toes!

31st January 2024: I had a very long, stressful time today as I was trying to type an answer to my brother. He sent an email to Maggie's (cancer help) help thing about me getting to Dundee etc. It was a really lovely email and so nice of him to help but I am very tired, stressed and trying to answer him when I can't really use the computer very much. In the end I decided it would be better and nicer to phone him. (I never use phones much as I am usually much better with emails etc). The phone call really helped, and we had a good old chat.

But trying to type, first of all, I had been on the computer for a few hours. I should have been relaxing today as I have Dr Who tomorrow. But now I can't stop thinking about Dundee again. My eye is twitchy. I have a mouth ulcer ridge. Actually, it has maybe been better for me to have written all this in the day rather than the night for a change. Maybe I will sleep better tonight. I am feeling a bit better already.

When I had my 3 weekly Dr Who's I could breathe easily through my nose at night for the first time ever, that I remember. The last couple of months and weeks it has been much worse again. My nose has no hairs in it. I got a bogie (excuse me) spot type thing for a while. Now that is all clear. The top half gets all blocked up, in the night. Vapour rub etc is starting not to work. In the morning, I have to clear out the gunk but there is also blood. I have had no more bleeding noses recently though.

They give me antihistamines, every Dr Who, I wonder if that is what is having an effect. I never have used them. It will be interesting to see how it goes, once Dr Who has stopped.

Babs has been so good listening and understanding. We have been going on wee walks round each week. She has gone and is going through so much and it is so nice to have her to talk to. I just don't want people and don't want to arrange times as I can't sleep for thinking about having to get up. I just need some rest, peace and quiet. But it is still so lovely to have her to talk to and be there for me. They all are, I know.

February 2024

1st February 2024: The oncologist, from Dundee, went through the treatment room, in Perth, a couple of times today. He says that it looks like, from the MRI scan, on Monday, that the lump has gone! ☺ ☺

The cannula worked fine today in my left arm. I am all bruised from Monday when they had trouble, they had to try both arms and two different ladies. They used the middle of my left arm. The lady said that it was rock hard all down my left forearm from the treatment. In Perth, they never comment much on such things. Last week, in Perth, they had to try both arms and two different ladies to get it to work. They ended up using my left hand, below my pinkie knuckle.

I think my hot flushes are back.

I asked the lady behind me, who was getting treatment, if I could turn the machine as it was driving me mad with the beeping. She said that was fine and that she was a bit deaf anyway. Without thinking, I replied, "oh that is handy"! What a terrible thing to say! I hope that she didn't hear me, but I suspect that she did. Sorry to that lady.

2nd February 2024: I haven't slept much. Perhaps because of the steroids? But doing good. I had a walk round the parks today. It is a lovely day but very windy.

It is fascinating that although it is the cancer that could very easily and very quickly kill me, it has not actually made me ill at all. It is the treatment, side effects and all the stress over all this time that has made me "ill".

4th February 2024: I have been awake since about 4am. I was in a bit of a strange state when trying to talk to Dad, on the phone, about Duncan's birthday meal at Delivino's. I couldn't really have a conversation or think. But I had a wonderful walk along Lady Mary's on Saturday, for ages. I saw waxwings on the way home. Nature and fresh air are, most definitely, my best medicine in the whole world.

My left arm is all bruised from Dr Who and the MRI on Monday. My right hand has a bad red rash.

My nose is blocked at nights. The body hair from my lower legs and toes is going.

I came across an interesting page on the internet by Pete Wharmby (Neurodiversity Speaker and Writer) I really liked what he said about autistic and non-autistic inter communication. That it is like an Apple and Microsoft computer. They are very alike, do the same job, and are the same thing but they don't work the same.

It was very interesting, when listening to him talk on the video, that I could listen easily and not get bored nor lose track of what he was saying. Usually, I find it difficult to just listen to someone just talking, it takes a lot of concentration, and I often get sidetracked. I am not sure that what he was talking about fitted the female side of autism so well, but it was still interesting.

(There is another new word or saying, "neurodiversity", that I don't like. I just don't like change especially when it is a new word that is suddenly used by everyone, and I really don't know what it means and if it is used, when a word that I do know used to be used. I find that very confusing, unsettling and never really use the new word. Except maybe, after a number of years when I am used to it, then of course, it is changed, and I don't want to change it!

I thought I better find out why people have started saying neurodiversity instead of autism. Interestingly, it is all about the positive aspects of all our different ways and saying how we are different, moving away from the medical type thoughts of something being wrong and needing fixing. So, all positive ideas and ideas that I agree with and have discussed in my book, *Answers Inside Out*. But can't we just change the thoughts, beliefs and ideas, without changing the name? I bet there are quite a few other autistic people who don't like names for things changing.)

5th February 2024: 4.10 am It's too much, this once-a-week treatment. I just need to get through two more. I need left alone, in peace and quiet. I can't think. I get on so great. I love everyone and everything. But I just need to be left alone. I don't want left alone.

There is something wrong. I always needed my sleep, even missing one hour took me ages to recover from. Now I don't want another letter, another day away with another appointment, to have to ask someone to take me. I just want peace and quiet. I am awake and I want to sleep. I will meet Babs. I love meeting her, but I don't want to plan a meeting. I knew this would happen. I am wide awake. I can't do this; I need to sleep. Something is wrong. I can't write this in case someone sees it.

I need to sleep. I love sitting out in the world of nature. It is so magic. I get lost in the magical, natural world. I don't have to think, I can just be. I love them all, but it is too much. Just two treatments to go, once a week, just leave me alone. But I love them all so much. I don't want to lose Babs; she is so wonderful. Duncan, Dad, Sue, Dolores, Helen, all of them.

I love them. I am so lucky to have their love. I can't write this in case anyone sees it.

There are so many others too. Diane, Chris, Findlay, Calum, all, all but I don't have time to do this. I want to sleep. I want to shut off. I need to sleep. People will want to see me, talk to me and I can't think. It is like I am split in half, down the two sides of my body. Brain processing is too much. I need to be left alone. The autism is massive.

It is great to write this, to get it out. It is incredibly therapeutic. I would never have done this. It really is Dr Who **Regeneration**. It doesn't matter if I am tired. But it does when someone wants me to do something. When I have to go to the shop, and I can't think what I am doing. I know it is wrong, now, when I get the medicine taste in my mouth. My tummy is tight up both sides. It is too cold with my baldy heed, but I have the window open as I am so hot, stuffy and can't breathe. There is a chill on my neck. I can't get a bug, get sore. I have sore knees, so I must be cold, but I am roasting. I am getting hot flushes again. My boobs are sore. I am now 56. I am scared that it is the menopause that caused the cancer, surely it should be over by now. It doesn't matter at all, but it is scary.

I have done nothing wrong, all natural things, but I got cancer. It is just a journey. It is so weird, fascinating and interesting. This is so silly; I should be sleeping. It is not silly at all. It is great to get it all out. I don't think we ever get things, thoughts, feelings all out. It is very good for you. Very healing. I love my salt lamp, it is beautiful.

I always thought people should not be up in the night but maybe they should. Do their own thing, what is right for them.

The back of my neck is too cold, my knees are cold, I will get sore. The poor world is so wild just now. The storm has been going on for days, for weeks. I love listening to the world, to the wind. It is singing, talking. It is healing. I love you, world.

My neck and knees are sore. I need to get warm. It is time to stop this, lie down, get my knees under the covers. But it is so good, so important. It is autism, I am getting this out. It is helping my head, the split.

I have put my lovely Snoopy blanket on, round my neck and over my head. Like E.T., phone home! Like some others with autism, I love the weight of my blanket on my head. I love my Snoopy blanket; it is one of my favourite things. It is so strange that I "met "my American friend, Ruth. (She is the one who gave me my Snoopy blanket. I have never actually met her, but we have corresponded for years and met in a synchronicity online site about the magic number 11.11.) But it is too much writing all this now. I need to go to sleep. Then I will lie with my thumbs and fingers going ,and write (in my head) whole letters, whole ideas, life, it all needs to come out, wants to come out it is such a waste, not needed.

(E.T. (E.T. the Extra-Terrestrial, 1982) was a film that I went to see in the cinema, with my cousin, when I was a teenager. It was a great film. We went to a cinema in Edinburgh and stood in a huge, long queue for ages and ages. They just got to about us in the queue when they said that the film was full. We wanted to see it and didn't want to lose our place, in the queue, so we stayed there until the next showing! That was a long wait, a few hours, to see the film. It was worth it though, in the end.)

I want to go to sleep. I have so much to do. But nothing to do. I want to do my painting for the Perth staff. It is such a waste of time writing this. I should be sleeping. It is a lovely warm blanket, but I am coughing now. This is so daft. I don't want to get ill. I need to get to sleep. I wonder if I am giving myself a bug. I have sore knees and am coughing. I need this out of me, but why? Why do my thumbs and fingers rub together? The world is so wild. The walls are creaking from the wind, the litter and bins are blowing and clattering about. My knee is sore. The world is so wonderful and magic. This is just rambling. I can't use this. I can't let anyone see this. It is a waste of time. I am so tired. But time does not exist. The world is blowing. The earth is healing. A car is zooming. Who is up at 4.39 am? Where are they going? Why?

This is so stupid as I will be so tired now. My nose is running. My window is wide open. It is so wild. I love fresh air. I love the world; it is so fresh. My knee is sore. That is it, I need to put the book and pen away but I have dropped the lid of the other pen. If I leave the book out, I might start writing again. Shush. Sleep.

I knew that this would happen and all because a friend asked me to meet them for a walk! It is lovely. I want to, she says I can leave it, but I don't want to. I don't want to let her or anyone down. I love them. It is just too much. I just need to be left alone.

My head goes round in circles. This is what my nephew does, did. They should never have given him medication. Autism needs space and quiet.

My head, my brain is split. This flowing. It is coming from somewhere else, another part of my brain. What is it? This is automatic, magic, spiritual? No, it is just from me, but it is a flow. Is this what it is like to be able to do things without thinking? Without autism? What is autism? What has the Dr Who done to me? Has it changed my brain processing? Oh, it is all so wonderful, so weird, so magic.

I am going to sleep now. Go away pain, it is sleep time. I need to put this away.

I am back now. I went to blow my nose, there was a big lump of gunk, snot, I had to put the light on. Get my big spotty hanky. I love my big spotty hankies. They are my cuddly. I shouldn't put the light on. It will wake me up. Now it is off. I couldn't see for going to the loo to get rid of the "snotty" thing. I am so tired now. I don't know what I am writing.

I have put my Snoopy blanket away now. I am cold, aching at the back of my neck, burpy and a tight tummy. I am so tired. I am daft, daft, daft. I am hungry. I can't think. I will be more and more tired, that will stress Dad. He doesn't understand about the tired. I can't explain, cause him stress. I don't want to. Duncan asked the Maggie people for help. That was lovely but he said he was so worried about Dad. That made me feel so bad, so sad. He was being helping, loving and caring.

I am in a strange state. This is coming out, but it is not me. I am detached and clear. This is weird. My head is weird. It is sleeping time.

Morning, I am up, and it is 9 am.

It is the autism. A lot of people don't seem to think that I have it, nor understand it as, I did so long just fine. It is not a thing that you can see. I write the books, but I think that maybe, only the ones who process things the way that I do can understand so much. Which is understandable. One friend doesn't seem to believe it. He says I don't have the lack of empathy.

It is so exasperating. I think that I have explained all about the differences between male and female autism, but I must just know and have not explained it enough. I think that people must know, because I do. That is not good teaching. It is like a driver thinking that you will know, automatically, the basics. It is also such a massive subject even with the males, it is so stereotyped. As I learn more and more about it, I forget that others don't.

Anyway, it is like the Dr Who has made my autism massive. It has really lowered the stress bar by miles.

It started two weeks ago (or more) with the Dundee appointment. We were late, I couldn't run etc. Then another visit to Dundee and trying to write my feelings in an email.

Then before I knew it, it was Thursday again so the next Dr Who. Then not having had sleep.

Also, everything is now all changing and vague again. The NHS know that I have autism but have no idea, time or it is not their job to think what change and unknown might do. That is **not** their job. (They all do incredible and such brilliant jobs.)

The appointment lady **did** make my appointment with the surgeon in Perth this time. Which is brilliant and lovely. I just don't want any more letters, appointments, no more having to ask someone to take me, organising, or thinking.

I am meeting, briefly, a friend on Monday. I have an appointment on Tuesday. Monday needs to be free. Now I have not slept again. I am up, as I want to get on, but I am in a daft state, again. It will soon be Thursday and Dr Who **again**.

I had a brilliant walk round with Babs and a great chat. She is so lovely and brilliant. It really does help to talk. Especially to someone who knows me better than anyone.

I am so sleepy. The Perth lady phoned for my telephone assessment, while I was out, I have to phone back. I don't like to disturb them; they are so busy. I phoned again and they said that Susan would phone back. So that is a better way, rather than me having to try to get through to them.

6th February 2024: It was the appointment, in Perth this morning., to talk to the surgeon, Sue took me. I gave blood in Perth too, to make it easier, rather than having to go to the Health Centre first.

It was the lovely lady that spoke to me on the phone and the surgeon is lovely too. It was really nice of them to give me an appointment in Perth, that is so much easier.

The lump is now only 7mm, as seen from the ultrasound. I suspected that it was still there, even although it looked like it was gone from the MRI. Perhaps that is because of the type of lump. It is worrying, for me, to think that means that it doesn't show up on scans. I wonder why it shows up on the ultrasound.

I am to get a number of weeks of healing after the chemo. Then my operation, in Perth. The whole area, where the lump was, is to be removed, some lymph nodes and they will also remove the 1st and 2nd markers that they put in. Then more healing. Then radiotherapy. I feel better now as I know a bit more about what is to happen and the timelines. I can't deal with vagueness.

I got a sick note from the doctor. I phoned last week. It ran out on Monday. I tried to phone today but there was a queue, so I left it. I am glad that I did, as they got back to me later on. I have written a wee note and will send it to HR (Human Resources) tomorrow. I have three more months off, for now.

We are so lucky with our wonderful NHS. I heard, on the news, last night, that King Charles has cancer. I had to switch it off. It was too miserable and went on too long, they should not make these types of things into a show, but it is very sad news. I can't deal with sad or bad things at all, even more so just now.

It is a lovely Spring like day. It is sunny, with a blue sky and beautiful. I went a wee walk round when I picked up my sick note.

I had a good sleep last night. That is the first time in about a week (apart from Friday), since going to the MRI scan in Dundee. I so needed some sleep. I just can't think or process anything. I get the medicine taste in my mouth, my sides go tight and sore, and I just can't think, to speak to or deal with people. I get on brilliant on my own though and had a brilliant, magical walk on Sunday (see my See Salt Tears: *Extras from Book* page 4th Feb 2024). I went to Lady Mary's, it was rainy, I sat and watched the birds it was so wonderful. That is the best medicine I could get ever, being out in nature and the fresh air.

When the health centre phoned to say that my sick note was ready, they also said that there was a note from the doctor to say that I could have an appointment to have a chat, if I wanted to, as I hadn't spoken to them for ages. But that I didn't need to, if I didn't want to, and if the hospital was looking after me. I thought that was so nice of them and it gave me faith in the now, very different and changing way that the doctors etc work.

It is brilliant that they give us a free lunch at the treatment.

7th February 2024: I have just been making a homemade quiche. It took me about 2 hours!! I don't know how people used to cook and do everything all day; it must have taken them ages and have been so much work. Now we just pop to the supermarket. I know it will work lovely and be very tasty. It is sausage quiche. It smells lovely. It is nice and good fresh ingredients for me.

See, I can't be so daft. I really do feel that it is just dealing with people that I can't do, just now. I am still very tired though. Mind you I have just forgotten about that, by getting lost in my cooking. It is very therapeutic. Now I mustn't forget to take it out the oven at 3pm.

I was thinking, this morning, about the lump and why I have it, if it will just come back, especially as it is a different kind. Why it doesn't show up in the scans and only the ultrasound. After a lot of thought, I once again realised that it is a journey. I don't have to fight or get rid of the lump, what they do to me, the treatment, dying, living or anything. What will be will be. I just am and just have to live the journey, whatever it is. Have trust and faith.

8th February 2024: It was the second last (all going well) Dr Who today. It went well. A bit chaotic at times, in the room, but a good day. I got home before 4 pm.

I am very burpy and a bit of burning coming up tonight. I am awake but not too bad. My thumbs and fingers are going. I want to get my painting done for them. (See **Unfinished Painting** part of the My Journey through Cancer page, on my *See Salt Tears* website.) I don't know if it is going to work, I am trying out my new gouache paints. I like using them, but they are a bit dull and stay too wet to work on top of. I am not patient with such things.

The oncologist, from Dundee, was there again. He said that he hadn't thought that they would get me anywhere near through all this, because of how I was at the beginning. He said I had done really well. People just really don't know about all that is going on, hidden, inside of the head of an autistic person.

I have a sore left arm in the night from the cannula or the treatment. I will try to get it better before Thursday, so that I can still use my right arm for drawing. I love my drawing; it is very therapeutic.

9th February 2024: I was doing hunky dory and lovely but then got the letter for my appointment in Dundee it is to be on 22nd Feb at 3.45pm. I tried to phone and make it earlier, but they couldn't change it. So, I phoned Dad to let him know. He, very nicely, said that it was okay and that he would take me. He then asked if I had any heart stones as he wanted to post some heart stones on his blog. I said I had one painted one and some crystals. But he wanted his heart stone to be in the same photo. I said that his stone was there and mine were here. He said that I could get his on Saturday and then take the photo. But I just can't cope with thinking about and planning or changing my routines in any way. I didn't want a lift home with his stone, then I would have to bring it back.

It sounds so daft. But I just can't cope at all with people or any changes to my world. I have told them, I have said that the autism line is so much lower, and they know that I have gone through 6 months of chemo, which has made my head not work. They also know I can't sleep, if I am stressed. But I really don't think anyone, really understands what I mean. In fact, lots of people say how it all seems to have gone so quickly.

I started roaring and jumping about, when on the phone, much to Dad's shock and surprise. In a wee minute, I had calmed down and he said, "good". After that I had a pain in my chest, my eyes were much worse etc. It is incredible how the slightest wee thing can affect me. I am now so tired. I was doing great today, before the phone call. Now I have got Dad coming down, this afternoon, and I have asked him to let me know when he is on his way. I can settle, after that, but it has given me a headache and my tummy and sides are tight, again.

(My poor Dad, he has been so brilliant and patient with, and for, me throughout this whole journey. Thank you, "Poppy".

10th February 2024: It is 4.11 am. I will be so glad to get off these steroids. I wonder if it will really affect me, badly, in a physical way. I don't think so. I think it might just really help me to sleep better. But is also just dealing with people too. I just need this all to be over for that, I think. If it ever will be?

At the moment, my autistic bar is so low. I was roaring and stomping my feet when I was on the phone to Dad, yesterday. It was just because he wanted me to take a photo of the heart stone that he had there and mine here. My head and thoughts just couldn't cope with that. I couldn't deal with waiting and change.

It is like the limbo bar, from when I worked at the kid's club. Or when we were to arch up like a cat in gymnastics at school, I just couldn't work it out. The teacher had to come along and physically move me, to show me what to do and I still couldn't do it. The level at which my autism shows itself is so much lower than usual. It is like that bar is only a foot above the ground and I could never get under it, **when** it was a metre higher than that!

I haven't slept for two nights. I am absolutely buzzing with, I think, the steroids. But I think that I wrote that letter to the oncologist, before my treatment started? And I was awake, then, for nights, planning, writing and thinking about that. Which suggests it is more to do with stress, change and autism.

11th February 2024:

(See Video Diaries on *See Salt Tears* Website 11th February 2024)

I had a wonderful walk and sit down by the river today. I saw a dipper and a woodpecker.

I wrote a wee poem today for my favourite hill, Turleum:

> *Turleum Hill, where have you gone?*
> *I can't see you.*
> *I know you're there. I know you're strong.*

See Salt Tears

My photos showing my favourite Turleum Hill vanished behind the fog and then it is back again with blue skies.

12th February 2024: Dad phoned to tell me about Mairi, my sister-in-law, today (she now has breast cancer). It is so sad and horrible. Strangely, it has made me calmer about things. We all have a journey to live. That is what we have to do. I believe, I have trust and faith. No matter what happens we get on with it. Suddenly I can look at all the photos of all the people and know that it is okay. We all die. We just get on with what we have to do. Now it is time to just get on with and enjoy life. I will also love all.

Okay thinking about it, this morning (with time) I know that Mairi does not need me to give her wise words of wisdom, nor to say I am sorry. I know and trust that, no matter what her journey is, she will be wonderful.

I wrote more here, as I was working through my thoughts and feelings, but they had details of Mairi's journey and that is her story to tell, not mine. So, I will leave that out.

I got my operation appointment letter for 28th February, one day less than two weeks from the last Dr Who! I thought that I would have longer to heal. Still, it will be hunky dory. It is great that it is to be with the nice man, surgeon, that I have talked to in Perth.

I phoned up to check about it, as it seemed so strange. Oh, that is so much better. They have phoned me back, after checking, and it is to be 20th March. Giving me much more time for healing.

One of the funniest things about all this Dr Who, is that I still have hairy lower legs and toes! The only hair that I might have wanted to get rid of!

15th February 2024: It was my **last** Dr Who today! ☺ Brilliant. I got to ring the bell. I can't believe I have never seen that bell before. I have passed it every time I have gone into the place.

See Salt Tears

I got flowers and the juice that I like, from Babs and Graham. I have put the flowers in the special owl vase that she gave me for Christmas.

The windows were not done when I got home. (I had arranged to get the leaking, broken windowpane and 2 others, in the stairwell, replaced. They were supposed to have done it while I was away at my treatment.) I thought it might have been my daftie, head getting muddled. But I have managed to check, and the money came out the bank fine. So, I must have done it right. I will just have to have trust and faith, being not doing. ☺

I did an <u>owl</u> picture today, during my treatment. It was magic and special. I got to use my right arm. It was my mum, saying hello. (I love owls and feel that they have a connection with my mum, for various reasons.) I heard an owl last night when I was in bed. I also saw catkins as we were going past Tesco's today. (Mum loved catkins.) I know that mum was with me and saying hello today. I love you mum.

I heard the owl again, tonight, before going for my bath.

I asked Letitia about the nose blockage and why the antihistamines, that they give me during the treatment, don't stop that and if it is just the burn and damage from the chemo. She said that not all things are from allergies. I asked her about my sore mouth with bad receding gums and it being very dry. And whether the special mouthwash that they give us to help with the pain, actually makes those things worse. She said to ask my dentist as I can go back to see him now. That they would give me advice. It seems pointless to go to the dentist who can't do any invasive stuff because of my treatment. My gums are bad, but my teeth are fine, I think. She said to give it three weeks and then let them know, if it was still bad. I hope that means that it might improve.

I am reading a book that my brother, Chris, gave me: *Strong Female Character* by Fern Brady. It is a great book and fascinating. It has made me think of things that I want to write about, but they are not relevant to this book. Maybe I will keep them for another book. It is difficult for me to do that as I just want to write everything.

In the car, today, Dad asked me if I was writing my book. I replied that I was taking notes but not writing it yet. I told him the name that it is going to have but have not told anyone else yet.

There is a very strange clicking and screechy music sound coming from the wall. I think that it must be the new neighbours. Oh dear, I can't cope with that in the night. They are very lovely and quiet, but the clicking is very annoying. I have put my ear to the wall, and it is like Bollywood music or something. To be fair, they have not made any noise at all yet. They are fine, just the strange scratching, oh dear. (I never heard that again after a while. We are so lucky with all the neighbours just now, they are lovely. We have had such trouble over the years.)

I am in a bit of a strange state today. Time seems to be a bit strange. I was expecting the book that I am reading (*Lord of the Rings*) and the news on tv, to fit in with and know what is going on with me somehow. I am quite disappointed in a strange kind of way when the book does not know to be wise about it. (I have no idea what I am meaning there, but I have written it to show you the strange kind of state that my head was in. A thing which other people couldn't see nor know about.)

The noise has stopped, he was singing. That was lovely but just not the clicking, whatever that was. I will be waking up thinking that there are mice again. But it has stopped, so that is brilliant.

He's got hours and nights of me burping, coughing, up to the loo, farting etc and then my music during the day. If they can hear all that!

I can feel liquid coming down my nose during the treatment. Letitia didn't seem to know what I meant when telling her about this. I am burpy and feel the burning up in my throat tonight. My thumbs and fingers are going but it is only 10.58 pm just now, so that is okay.

I am in a strange state. I think it is wrong to write all these things, I don't want to upset Findlay (my brother). I don't want to upset anyone, but I think with the book etc that it is a strange mix and somehow all connected. (Again, I don't know what exactly I was wanting to say here but am writing it to show how my head and feelings were all in a muddle.)

11.53 pm: I have been trying not to write this, but my thumbs and fingers are going. I only slept last (Wednesday) night, since last Thursday and now I am back to the steroids again. It is okay though I just have to get past this week. hopefully.

I fell the burning coming up in my chest and liquid going down my nose.

I was freezing so put the blanket on, but then I get roasting, so have to take it off again.

Time is wrong again. There was a second lady next to me today in the treatment room. I knew she was in the seat and saw her going to the loo but (it must have been) not long after that, I got very confused as she came out of the loo, and I had forgotten all about her being there. I also remembered that an older lady was on that seat, but I looked over and the second lady was there again. I was very muddled and yet I talked away to them fine. The first lady, suddenly, earlier, was unplugged from the machine and plaster on, ready to go.

Oh, my goodness what a muddle these sheets of paper with my notes will be in. I will have to try and put them in order, like a jigsaw!

17th February 2024: I've had a lovely day. Duncan and Fergus (Duncan's Scotty dog) were here, for his birthday. Dad took us all to Delivino's with the Christmas token that he got from Sue. Delivino's is my favourite restaurant. My tummy is not working yet but I still enjoyed it. I had sausage pizza and chips. I should have asked for veg. (I never like if I get a meal without vegetables. We always had to have vegetables with our meals at home. I didn't like that, sometimes, but it is a rule and now I find it "not right" and very surprising when, I am somewhere, and they don't give you veg with your meal.) I had pudding (dessert) but it was cold which was really sore on my mouth. It got better. I am going to carry on with the mouthwash for this week.

I told Dad and Duncan about the owls and mum being with me on Thursday. Duncan said that my niece talked to a medium. I have been waiting for a sign to find the right medium. Hearing this, just after saying about mum, is a real sign. I am going to ask my niece about the details.

Why is cancer called cancer? I never liked that word. I didn't know I had a problem with it. If I ever talk to someone, I have just tapped my boob and said, "I have a lump". I never liked the star sign being called cancer.

I watched a good film about a doctor and his son going to the mountains for a holiday.

11.04 pm: I should get to sleep. My thumbs were going while I was watching the film. It is the last day of the steroids.

I had a synchronicity today. I was looking at the loads of mole hills on Callum's Hill up at their house (my dad's). I was talking to Sue about how I had never seen anything about moles on anything. Then this evening, on my Facebook feed, was an underground book, with a mole in it.

I feel wide awake.

Duncan gave me a pack of organic camomile for herbal tea.

1.49am: I was just up to the loo and didn't want to put the light on, but my thumbs started, and I just wanted to say about the windows.

I got a quote, and they said they would fix the windows on Thursday. I was at the hospital, but it didn't matter as it is in the stairwell, so I didn't have to let them in or anything. It was to cost nearly £400. I decided to get it done anyway, for the sake of the flat.

But when I got home from the hospital, I was really scared that it had all been a con when I saw that they hadn't been done. However, I decided, in the night, to just have trust and faith and left it.

I thought that I must have done the bank transfer wrong. A day or two later, I got the ladies email that they had received my money. I replied oh thank goodness I had had a panic when I had seen that the work had not been done. She checked and said that the job had been done! Panic, back! I replied, "Oh My God, I really don't know what to do now, as my windows were n**ot** done. Luckily, I had sent them photos of the windows and the flat door, in the first place. After a few emails back and forward I got put to the boss. He reassured me that I don't have to pay for the ones that were done by mistake! It turned out as a lovely story, as a neighbour, who doesn't know, has had a magic fairy fix their broken windows!

I have slept up until now, I woke, or I think I woke from thoughts, a dream (?) about Amazon Prime asking my opinion about all the things that I would like them to think, note and ask. The real things that matter to me about my new and old Kindle. The adverts, which are new in Amazon Prime Video. The mix, discovery etc in Prime Music. How I listen much more but am skipping a lot of songs. Oh, the strange things that my head tries to sort out and think about, while I should be sleeping.

The COOP stopped us saving our money on our Member's Cards. They said, we listened to you". Well, they didn't listen to me, as I didn't want them to stop that.

I am a bit farty now. Is that my tummy starting to work? The back of my leg is a bit sore and feeling like the blood is not flowing. I put my lavender gel on it. My throat and chest are feeling a bit funny. I now need to settle back down. I had a bad taste a few times today. The back of my shoulder is a bit uncomfy from sitting wrong, I think.

I booked a thing off Facebook today. It says it is a free art class, for a week in March. It seems real. I hope it is real. It will be interesting to see, if I do it, what it is like. Maybe it is a con, as now Facebook is showing a few of those free do this and that business type things. But it seems good. I have noticed, these last few weeks or so, that my Facebook feed has been much more interesting. My brother, Duncan, has noticed that too. Maybe it is starting to work better. Maybe they are listening instead of all those fashionable, greedy changes? I will have to have trust and faith. Perhaps the magic of thought, of being, not doing, really does work. ☺

There is a wasteland just along from the flat, where they demolished an old hotel. I always wanted to buy the old falling apart building, take it down and create a nature garden, on the site. Now it is all overgrown. I have sneakily thrown a few wildflower seeds on there. There was an article in the local newspaper that the owners must tidy up the site by January. Well, that didn't happen. I will maybe take a photo of it. Maybe I will get my wildflower garden after all.

Duncan told me about Maggie's charity, well that was another synchronicity. The book that I gave him for Christmas, amazingly had the garden that is next to the one that he works in, in it. What is more, is that, apparently, it was created by Maggie's husband. The open day charity that Duncan does for his work, each year, is collecting money for Maggie's

Cancer Care and it has nothing to do with him what choice they make, it is his bosses' choice.

Duncan said that Maggie's had got back to the message that he wrote to them, about me. They said that it would be better if I contacted Maggie's myself and that it would be the Dundee one. The idea of that just makes my tummy go wonky but he understood. I just can't deal with new, unknown things, nor having to contact Dundee, in case I would have to go there. He understood. I just can't think about more Dundee things, nor going to a group or anything like that. Well, I can get back to sleep now?

My pen ran out. Thank you for letting me write all this. It is brilliant. It gets my thoughts out. Which really helps. I think it is like talking away to someone. My therapy?

I need to lie down. I will put more stuff (it is natural, essential oil rub for muscle aches) on the back of my shoulder. I am sitting wrong and getting sore.

2.14 am Just one more thing . . . My second pen ran out . . . got a third one . . . Sue has been saying to me, over the past few months, "don't shout". She really jumps. I think that I might be going a bit deaf from the Dr Who. But also, the steroids are making me strange and hyper or maybe it is stress and a strange state from the lack of sleep. It reminds me, a bit, of when my nephew, Jack, suddenly shouts. I am doing that to Babs sometimes too. But also, Dad is quite deaf now and so I shout, a lot. Sometimes, when he puts his hearing aids in, he says, "you don't need to shout".

2.35 am My thumbs are going too much, and my eyes are starting to twitch. I had to start more writing. So, I am onto the blue notebook now. I have put my pillows up a bit, to help with my shoulder. I had two or three things to say but I don't know what they were now. That is not good, as they will come back again. I am very tired now. I notice that my eyes feel really sleepy when I wake up too early. But I feel a bit allergic today. I was sitting down on the floor, talking to Fergus, a lot. He is so lovely. Granny used to say that I got my allergies bad when I used to sit on the floor with Beth (our family dog). I put Optrex in my eyes this evening, a lot.

I have remembered one of the things, as I was writing this, but have forgotten it again! I really don't want to stop writing, put the lamp off, then have to put it back on again.

18th February 2024:
It was a beautiful day; I had a wonderful walk. I saw a red squirrel and goldfinch. See the photos on my *See Salt Tears* website, Extras from Book page (18th February 2024).

I was in a strange state this afternoon. I am very tired, more tired, on my walk, than expected. I sat for a long time watching the world and its magic.

I think that the weekly Dr Who's are more like the three weekly ones than I thought. It seems that about every three weeks, I feel more affected or there are new effects. The rash on my hand is bad. It was so exciting and on a high to finish and ring the bell, that I had expected to be brilliantly better. I was forgetting that I have just had my treatment, have changed my routines and had Duncan's visit. I haven't slept. Also, my hard drive, that had all my videos on it, has stopped letting me put things on it. Usually, I would try and work out how to sort that, no matter how long it took. So, I tried to do that this afternoon, not stopping when it was just too much.

Dad phoned wondering if he was taking me somewhere this week. I had Thursday all planned for Perth and Dundee. I think it was really, just all crammed up on the calendar, so Dad wasn't sure, but it got me stressed as I had to think, and I was scared that my plans would change. Again, my autism is so much more emphasised. I don't usually deal well with change, especially when I have something all planned, but it is so much worse for me to deal with just now, even just the thought of it.

I put the computer off and then the television off, for tea. I am writing this now. But I will try the computer again now. I should have just left the hard drive thing. I have loads of time to heal now. I just have to remember that the treatment was on Thursday, and this is only Sunday.

The oncologist talked to me when he was in the room in Perth. He said that he never thought that they would get me through this, with what I was like at the beginning. He then said, "and that is all down to you, doing so well." Of course it was also all the wonderful staff, Dad, Sue, my friends and family. But it was a lovely thing for him to say. He also said, at the beginning, that by the last few treatments, they sometimes have to stop, as people have just had enough. So, I just have to remember that this is still just the last one and it was only a couple of days ago, with plenty more unknowns and stress still to come.

I am still thinking about and planning Dundee, for the radiotherapy. What will happen to me and what if it comes back? Right, I will go and try the computer now. Oh, my goodness, I am so tired.

My tummy is full of food from yesterday (a family day) and since Thursday.

Oh, now my Facebook comments are not working right, and I can't comment as B's Photos, to reply. I know it doesn't matter and will change or sort itself soon, I expect. But it is making my tummy go worse. I don't want this to be all moans, but it is important to show the stress and its effects.

Oh, that is better, I just had to comment in a different way, and it worked. They are obviously updating and changing things. But I do think some of the changes are better. I don't think that I need to write all this, especially not all in one day. It is just me talking and getting my troubles out. I will still do it, as it is therapeutic, but I may leave it out of the book. The night thoughts and writings are important though.

See Salt Tears

This is a very long troubled, muddled, load of writing, from a long night, but by the morning I had had a massive break through. Enlightenment and answers, complete regeneration for me. So, stick with the negative to get to the positive, brilliant.

I think it is my autism that makes me like the truth but also makes me enjoy a world of escape. (Particularly, apparently for some females with autism, we can create a world of escape and fantasy) Suddenly this has hit home. Trying to not think about it (the cancer) is my way of dealing with it, fantasy. Which works, if no one else is involved. Tonight, I am so tired. I have read that same line and page, in *The Lord of The Rings* for ¼ hour. Then, waking up as doing that! I am so cold. I have put my favourite Snoopy blanket on the bed, my comfort. I don't like change, my way of being in control but this journey has all been, completely out of my control. I am to have trust and faith, that is all I can do. I am paranoid tonight, that I have said things wrong, that might hurt people. It is time in life when I need to think more about looking after Dad and Sue. I just can't do change. Even Babs needs looking after but is having to look after me.

I have become disillusioned with some men. I've put them on pedestals, but it was my old way to flirt (ha that sums up an image that is not me at all), it doesn't work, as it means nothing. They can have fun but now it means nothing, an old life, an old way.

I have been hiding away, all these years, as it all means nothing. I have been happy in my own world. I am now in the menopause and years when men are not interested. I don't know what I am going on about, they never were. Yes, they were, but only for excitement and fun. They didn't see, know, want me. Well, why am I blaming them? It is me who wanted, craved love and attention. Nothing to do with men or anyone. I just wanted care and love but also freedom. It is such a strange world of dreams and fantasy, autism for females. I need care, warmth, comfort, no change, stability but also need to be so alone and distant. So, I have learned how to do both but don't know that I have done this. I always was strange or different. Now, no one can help me with this (the cancer). I have to do what they (the medical people) say. I can't control it but if I just have trust and faith, and I can do that, until others are involved, as I don't ever want to hurt others. It must be so much harder to do this with children or a partner. The people, who have that, can't just hide away but then maybe; it is also easier? Thousands, millions, billions of people, have been through so much worse.

I am paranoid today that I signed up to a con, with that art thing that I clicked on online, from Facebook What does it matter? What does any of it matter? That is why, maybe, I went tough. I became a tomboy, when I was young, as then I could be left alone or could pretend, it was all a pretence. I don't know who I was. I can just be me, on my own, in my own world. I have to have trust and faith in others. Oh, I need to be quiet now and stop writing and just think. That is what I used to do before all of this. The writing down is too much. What if you all find it? Well, it can't matter then. It is said but it is all rambles. Our insides are **not** meant to come out. Now let me think and stop writing. Thank you, goodnight.

I am going to miss the Perth people so much in some ways. They asked how I was, each week, looked after me. Helped, did everything for me, even gave me my lunch and yet it was all with stuff (treatment, chemo) that I didn't want. But it was to make me better. So confusing. All so strange.

4.51 am: I was really freezing; I had that last week as well. I wonder if it is a stress thing.

I just realised a connection, the name, Dundee, is causing me so much stress. The thought just planning, can't think etc. But I have just realised it is like a big circle. I tried to leave home (after school); it all went wrong and has very unsorted and unlooked after, connections in my head. Terrifying. Sue painted, cleared out my room, all was put away and I was at Dundee and lost. I came home but just argued with Dad. I haven't lived at home since that Christmas. I moved in with

Tom (our good family friend). I had a bottle of Martini (from the girls in the student flat at Dundee), I drunk it all and then went to meet Babs. She had to go to work, so took me on the bus with her, I got the bus home again and ever since then, about 40 years ago, I have never kept alcohol in the house. I pretended to be grown up. I was unemployed, Sandra (Babs' sister) helped a lot. Babs' whole family have been my extra family.

Sue has an appointment, needs someone to care, listen. Dad is at home; I don't know if he knows about the appointment. That is bad communication, but I can't get stressed at all. I need to stop. I should go up tomorrow and ask but I can't think (I did go and had a good chat with Sue). I need more time to rest, heal, think. I need to, maybe, just say this, leave it in the book, but is all about me. I can't talk or think. It is so interesting, all this. Lack of communication, that is the trouble with most things in the world, or rather society. Well, that is interesting, I have just realised that there is this massive, scary, leave home connection, but that is actually one of the best things I have ever done in life, we all need to, and it is natural.

(I went to Dundee, to study Architecture, for a term after I left school. It didn't work, I gave up and came home.)

I need to talk to someone about the Dundee thing, it is a big fear, an unknown. Maybe I could talk to the doctor? I am a bit stressed and can't cope with the unknown.

It is really bad and scary too about Mairi. Findlay needs support too and someone to talk to. I hadn't known just how bad we are at communicating, or I am. I just can't do this just now. I can't think. I need to sleep and heal. I don't even know what days Sue does what, with all her clubs and things.

I can't deal with this just now, but I need to think about it. It is daft of me, I think that I need to just stop, wait, heal and have trust and faith that things will work out. But Sue's appointment must be soon. I should ask. I think this is all my autism and Dads and all of us, except Sue, I suppose. And yet, I don't communicate, none of us do, much. It must be so sad and scary for her with Findlay. Dad is at home, not working, they will be grumping a bit at each other. She will be worried and thinking no one cares but I don't even know. I must ask. But I am too tired. It is all about me. Right now, it has to be. I just need time to heal, to think. Maybe I can try saying that. I have no one to talk to about any of this. I don't even know it myself until now that I am writing this. This can't be written in my book I don't think, but it is really helping, therapeutic. I can talk here; this will help me think and sort this out. But I need to sleep. Maybe I don't. Maybe if I just leave everything, the book, art, computer, just stop and take time to think, process. I am scared to talk to people, to ask, in case they say I have to go there (I don't want to have to go anywhere).

I found out that the owls that I am hearing, are actually oyster catchers, I think. Not owls at all. I love you mum. (I looked up info com when worried and up came owl nation. Very weird and wonderful synchronicity. Mum.) A parliament of owls was oyster catchers!

I can't think, help others, just now but I don't want to hurt or bother anyone. So, I will hide away, stay away, that is what I always do. But it is confusing now as people need help and communication. I just don't do that. I stay away and look after myself, but I can't just now. I need some help and have no idea how to get that nor ask for that. Everyone said that they would take me places, but it is all their times, their lives. I have never been able to fit in with others. I have to just look after myself. That is the only way that I can cope, do it, but now I can't. I don't as I can't travel. I can't drive or even think about it. My head couldn't do that just now. It is too terrifying and scary. I need to ask someone. But I just can't think of being out of control.

It is my autism; I need to get someone to help me to sort my head and thoughts out. I need to get to PRI (Perth Royal

Infirmary) each day. I need to talk to Dad, calmly, without getting stressed or angry, but he is getting muddled, and I am causing him stress. I really don't want to, it is so scary, he is in his eighties. I should be looking after him. But I can't even look after myself. Actually, I am, and I can, very well and thrive on my own. The only trouble is the getting to Dundee. That is the problem, the key. So just get me to PRI (Perth) and then I will get the bus, from there to the hospital in Dundee. It will only be for 1 month or less. I will talk to him and Sue. Ask them for help and advice. Trust them to help me. I don't want to be a bother. The whole of autism is, that I don't want to hurt anyone, be a bother, but people, including me, don't know that. I need to believe in and be myself. That is the only way for me to cope and deal with life but that doesn't work when I need to deal with the world.

It is now, **5.22 am**. I need to rest and sleep. Hopefully, writing and thinking about all this has helped. I am **very** stressed, have the tablet taste but I think that this has helped. I need to give myself this. I need to think, heal, but I need to talk to Sue. Maybe I should just leave it, being, not doing and see how I feel, have a day or two. I just had chemo. The effects have not stopped just because it is the last time. I need time to heal, to think. I can't talk, think about others yet. I am understanding the idea of a "mancave" more. They need time to think. Peace and quiet. It seems like they are not caring but they maybe are. Okay, it is time to put the lamp out and try to settle.

Okay, this has worked. It is all quite simple. ☺ There is no hurry. I have a week or more to heal, think, sleep, and be myself. Leave me in peace.

I will talk calmly and clearly with Dad, check that he is fine with taking me to Perth each day. I won't try to control or change that, but I don't have to think about that or worry just now. I have a month to heal, to focus on getting better. I will ask Sue about her appointment. I will wait a few days then try to send people some correspondence, but I don't need to do that now. I just need to focus on sleep, healing, have trust that

I will get to Perth and Dundee. I will let Sue and Findlay know that I am thinking about them, but give me a day or two, to sleep, heal, and think.

There is a whole month where I don't even have to think about this, but that doesn't work. Okay so no rush, be calm, stop, listen, and think. This is why my walks in nature help me so much. I need to be still, peaceful, quiet and alone. I have to remember to look after me. I can do that. I can do it. But then I am back in the cycle, the problem comes when I can't look after myself. When I need help. Well, I can look after myself. I just need to stop, listen and think. I just can't think of helping others, before I have stopped, thought and looked after myself. That is what I am forgetting, how to look after myself. I can't deal with others; this is so out of my control. Autism control, this was sorted, but now my tummy and middle are uncomfortable again. It is like Jack's (my nephew) cycles. The thumbs, the fingers, the repetition, the thoughts. The same thing, over and over, for hours. I am understanding so much more about Jack just now. My autism is just so much more. I need calm, peace and to be left alone and in control. Actually, it is all really fascinating. Okay I have a month before the operation, that is in Perth, so fine, I just need to take time to heal now. I know that I can get to Perth, so I can forget about it and have trust in that, for another, healing month. I can get from there to Dundee. Give me time to heal. Let Sue know I am thinking about her. I can't think but I realise she has an appointment.

Once I am healed a bit, this week, then I will send Findlay a message, I have sent Mairi my good wishes. I have to rest just now. I have loads of time. I should think of it like I have been ill and take time, spoil and look after myself, even although it is mentally ill, mind you, it is physical too. I need time to heal from the regeneration.

I think the park would be a good walk tomorrow. There is no rush to go to the house. I will give it a day, at least, for me to sleep and heal.

Circles. That is the problem. It, things just go round and round. I know now I have time, that I don't have to worry, but that is **not** stopping.

It is something about autism, worry, circles, cycles. Just going round and round. It won't shut up, the same things. I need to switch off. Stop, listen, and think. I know I don't have to think about this. I need to switch off. I can't do that, I can, I know the answer. Just stop, heal, listen, and think. Have trust and faith. I need to sort the problem, to be in control. But I have. I know that I can get to Perth. I know it is ages yet. I know that I can get to Dundee, cycles again. Back to the beginning.

Life is giving me a circle, a cycle. I will think about that. What is it telling me? Dundee started, art, Graham taking me there (Babs and Graham took me to Dundee, after school, when I first tried to leave home), talking about Mrs Thow etc. (Graham remembers things, really well, he was reminding me about my landlady, Mrs Thow, etc from when I first went to Dundee. This was on the day that he took me for my scan appointment). Leaving home. It has all been a massive cycle, change life and control, it is fascinating. I feel alone but that is how I thrive I have done it. Now it is time. Time for a new life for me. It is wonderful and magical. I have trust and faith. But I can do it. It is a whole new life. **REGENERATION.** Slowly, calmly, surely. Gently, slow. I can do this. It is magic, I have time, I have months. This is what I always wanted. Always needed. I am an author, artist and, and what is it? Author, Artist and what?

6.05am: Time to sleep. author, artist and?? Got it . . . photographer. Author, artist and photographer. Magic ☺ Have trust and faith. I can do it.

8.05am: Morning. My head is burning on the right-hand side. From all this thinking but I got to sleep from the 6.10 writings, I will try a wee half hour more.

Now I know to say that the autism does **not** go away just because people don't think you have it or don't see it or say things like, everyone has it a bit. It is here, real and I know that. That is **VERY IMPORTANT.**

19th February 2024: I and people like me can't talk or tell you things in the usual way. Can't, is not a good word but it just doesn't work that way. What I can do, is write and tell you, my story. I can write, nonstop, and tell all. That is why we, some of us, are so good at writing our story. It enables us. Is our way and ability, male, female and all.

That is why Aspergers was finding its voice, its power. **That should not and never be taken away.** Change the name of Aspergers but don't write **us** out of History.

It is most important to society. To read, listen, see and hear our stories. All of ours, everyone. It doesn't matter at all about grammar, correct English. Folklore is real life, words, our story, without the physical words.

It really is complete Regeneration, on all levels, physical, mental **and** spiritual. It is magic and incredible. **I love me.** We are **All,** so love me (yourself), is actually, love all. That is **the key**. The healing.

I don't have to run, go away. I am an Artist, Author and Photographer already. I always wondered what I would, could be. Well, I am.

I am home. I am me. ☺

Thank you me, all, so much for this journey. It is true enlightenment. ☀☺☘

20th February 2024: I slept well, I woke around 4am but it was a different kind of awake I was able to see my eye patterns and relax. I had a nice walk round.

My attempt to make oatcakes, like Duncan made, was a disaster. I couldn't finish them and had to give them to the birds!

I had a nice chat with Diane.

I am very tired for the computer.

It is a beautiful day.

I asked AI (Artificial Intelligence) and got the answer that the green medical mouthwash can cause sensitive gums. So, I am going to try to stop taking it. I have been using it for the last couple of weeks as my mouth has been so sore.

21st February 2024: For two nights, I have slept much better and in a different way. I was able to see my eye patterns and switch off again last night. I woke about 5.30 am but still got back to sleep.

(I mean the patterns that you can see behind your eyelids when you shut your eyes. I, in good times, watch them and that helps me relax and get to sleep.)

I keep saying to people about how I need time to heal, which is right. They think that the treatment is finished, so that is it. (Actually, that is what I think that they think, but they probably don't at all. It is me that says it to them.) It is brilliant that the Dr Who Regeneration is finished but it is still not a week. My system is still in treatment. It would have been another Dr Who tomorrow.

Something huge has changed. I think it has been the night (see 18th February 2024) or rather the morning after that night. When I worked out about me being home and already being an artist, author and photographer.

(I shouldn't say or write what people think. I can't know what they think. I can suppose. What I think they think is, I expect, a massive part of autism. Or rather my reaction to what I believe. I suspect it is actually, nothing like what I think. They are not focussed on me and have their own lives to live and think about. It is more what society, and our life experiences think.)

I have noticed, over this time, how people I meet just briefly in the street, seem, often, to talk about sad, negative things. I suppose that thinking of someone being ill, moves our thoughts to that. Also, it is our small talk (maybe just in Scotland but I don't think so) like we do with the weather. We want to talk about ourselves, our own experiences. I reckon we do that to try and help but it also seems to be a natural unconscious thing that we do.

I heard a lady talking to someone else, in the Dr Who room, a while back, after it was announced that King Charles had cancer. She was saying that it, cancer, was getting talked about so much in the media. She just wanted to get on with it (her healing and treatment journey) and not talk about it. I have been the same. It is easier to cope and get on, dealing with it, in that way.

People are not knowing me at all when they see me. Three people today and one the other day, that I have known for years. It is not just because I have my hat etc on. But I look very different. I have no eyebrows, eye lashes, am pale, have blotches on face and my shape has changed, slowly, I am a bit more swollen but also thinner in bits on my face and, also generally.

This has been handy at times, over this journey. I say hello or hiya (as we say here). There is then a silent pause as they obviously have no idea who is saying hello to them. I hear them saying hello as we move off. They are wondering who on earth is saying hello to them.

I went a lovely walk with Babs the other day. We went along to see the alpacas which are in a field not too far from here. They are lovely, characterful looking creatures.

Babs took a photo of me with the alpacas. I liked it. I haven't told anyone on Facebook about this journey, so have been very careful of photos in the last months. Although they must guess or wonder. But this alpaca photo was lovely, bright and cheery with the beautiful landscape, that we have around here, behind it and my favourite Turleum hill. So, I asked Babs if she would post the photo on my Facebook page for me. Which she did.

I had to laugh though, as with my smile, teeth and the angle that I am leaning at, I actually, look a bit like an alpaca in it.

Babs' photo of me by the alpaca field.
Please note my favourite hill, Turleum, in the background.

Ha, I think that I am calmer and better but, oh my goodness all these wise thoughts and words of wisdom and it has all unravelled completely with one tiny, unimportant, thing. The effect of autism is so vast and does not go away.

See Salt Tears

I just had the most completely wonky talk with Dad. He only phoned to say that we might park at Dobbies (a garden centre with a café) tomorrow, for lunch. Tomorrow (22 February 2024) is for my pre-op assessment, which is in Perth and then, later in the day, an appointment in Dundee to put the marker chip in for my operation. I have it all planned out, including what will happen for lunch etc, as usual and as doing that, really helps me. It is so good with Dad as he lets me plan and fits in and understands, which helps me so much.

Then he phoned to say about going for lunch at Dobbies, which was a tiny change in the plan. It would be much easier for him to park there. It was, however, a change to my plan and I couldn't cope with that. I felt it in my heart and my chest.

He said, it's fine and that we didn't need to change, that it was no problem and went off the phone but now I am so stressed and will have made him more stressed. Probably not, but it has made me so affected, from one tiny thing. I am so unsettled now. If I phone back later then that will get me stressed, again, thinking about it. It does not matter at all but now I am really bothered that I have made him stressed. It is incredible how affected I am. I really hope that this does not change my sleep back to not good tonight. I have my sore side and my chest is tight.

I will calm down now. Leave it. Say later, that Dobbies is a great idea, and it is! Oh, my goodness, how fascinating, how much a tiny thing, change, stressed me.

I know it doesn't matter at all. I need to calm down and get on with my healing day. I feel sick, have a sore side and am burpy. I get burpy when stressed.

I phoned him back and said that Dobbies is a great idea. Now I don't have to think about it as it is changed, and all is good. He seems fine, so it is back to my healing and playing my piano. Oh, my goodness, it is incredible just how much one wee change affected me. I have tired eyes and am feeling the burning coming up, etc.

I think that, perhaps, my further panic was more, subconsciously, to do with my shock at the reaction that I have and not wanting to stress Dad. But my involuntary going on about it, stressing him a million times more. He just wanted to go off the phone, but I had to sort it and make sense of it, for me This all happened automatically in a tiny amount time, subconsciously and not, in any way, rationally.

Some of my autistic reactions seem to be about others, myself but not wanting to upset others. It is ironic as I really, probably upset them much more, with the fuss. (Actually, I don't think they would even notice or know what was going on. Perhaps just now, on this journey, but never really, in normal times.) It is not a fuss; it is autism, and it is fascinating.

All that was with my calm, brilliant dad. Imagine if it was with a stranger. Mind you, it is only because I trust and can be myself with Dad. If it had been a stranger, then I would have waited until later. That sounds like I have a choice or control over my behaviour or reaction, I don't. It all happens in my subconscious. Perhaps masking, as they talk about, particularly for females with autism. It is part of my life, and I have always lived with it, without, until very recent years, even knowing that I had autism.

I am writing far too much about all this now. It is like that state that I have been in during the nights, but this has been in the day. Hopefully this will get it out of me, and I can calm down now.

A bit later on: I am much calmer now. I can't believe the fuss and weirdness that I made of that.

The sun is coming out. I have read and looked on Facebook about the crystal shop, it has a new name. My mind makes up so much. I have to trust and have faith. **(I don't think that this has anything to do with anything, in this book, but it shows how my head jumps and changes to something, completely different.)**

22nd February 2024: I have two appointments today, the pre-op assessment in Perth, then the ultrasound and marker clip inserted at Dundee. I have been awake from 2.30 until after 4am, but a good awake, much more relaxed. I am very tired. I had a nice walk round, as don't have to leave until 11.05.

Dad took me. The Perth appointment went well. There was a lovely lady and man, asking me questions, then checking my heart, blood etc. My right arm didn't want to give blood, but they got it from the left arm. They didn't use the belt like a band tourniquet; they used one like a rubber glove material. She said that they have to use them now, for cleanliness. I don't like them as they ping on and can cause bruises.

We then went for lunch at Dobbies. I had a delicious lasagne, chips, broccoli and peas. We then took our time looking round the garden centre and shop, to use up the time before going to Dundee.

We got there in good time and got a parking space much easier than usually, probably because it was later in the day.

On the ultrasound, I saw the lump (a black vertical rectangle on the screen). I could see the first marker in there. It is fascinating to see. There is lots of white that the lady said is tissue.

I thought that the marker was going to be shot into me, like the first one, but this one had to be pushed in. I was given a local anaesthetic. He then had to place it, right next to the original marker. It was quite uncomfortable. But he was having a big struggle to get it through whatever it was, the lump or tissue. He kept saying, "pressure" "pressure", I am glad that the lady was there, as she said, things like, "are you okay" and "this might hurt a bit". They were both lovely, again. Once it was in, he said, "we have to now test it". I hadn't realised that it worked by sound. It worked fine, there was a kind of clicking noise to show where the marker was. I asked if I would be setting that off, with things. The lady laughed and said, "no". I bet they get asked that a lot.

So, I am now like the crocodile in Peter Pan, who swallowed an alarm clock! They will take both markers out, during my operation.

I was surprised as I then had to go for a mammogram. I didn't think about getting one of them, as the lump doesn't show up in it, but it was to tell them whether the marker was sitting correctly beside the first one. If not, it would have to be moved. Luckily, it was sitting well. So, I got to leave. I have been in that place, a number of times now, but still always get muddled about the direction for getting back to the waiting room. The lady said I could go. Luckily, I got up to follow her, before she disappeared, as I was following her in the wrong direction again! She showed me the right way to go and so I found Dad again.

I can't walk too fast, yet. So, when Dad was hurrying back to the car, I said so. I hadn't realised how late it was getting, and he and Sue don't like driving in the dark now. We managed to get mostly back to Crieff before it got too dark. Now, later in February, we got home by 6. I had taken a picnic in case we had been longer at Perth. I was bothered by being late home for my tea (evening meal) and wasn't going to have very much, instead of eating my picnic. I don't like having a late tea and we had had a good lunch. But Dad said, as we went through Perth, that I could have my picnic and eat it in the car. I honestly hadn't thought of that. We laughed about that. I am so one for my routines, that it really made my day to get to eat my tea, at my teatime, and not have to bother about it or take up time when I got home. It made me so happy. Just a wee example of how much it helps me., particularly just now, to carry on with my routines.

I was awake about 3 am, in the night, but got back to sleep again like the last few nights. It is only one week since my last Dr Who Regeneration. My face is getting a bit blotchy, like the rash on my right hand but not nearly so bad. There is a spot bit above my lip and a rough bit in my right ear. But it really feels like I am healing a bit already. I was not allowed my bath last night or this morning. I so love my baths. I had to put my lovely Snoopy blanket on the bed last night to warm me up. I went a walk with Babs this morning.

I have been using the computer a lot, this afternoon, to try and buy an external hard drive as the one with my videos on it has stopped letting me write to it. I spent a few hours looking through all the reviews. I got a bit grumpy as I was going round in circles and wasting so much time. Which I have done already, other days searching for one. I finally chose one and have bought it. I am wondering whether the cloud might actually be a better idea, as Graham always tells me and everyone else seems to use. But I just feel that in the future they will charge us so much and that it will be like they own your things, photos, videos, documents etc. I really don't like that idea and am very suspicious of it.

So, having been looking at the computer for a long time, my eyes are very tired, and it has been too much, but again it is already better than before and I don't feel ill with it, just very tired. My mouth is dry, and my tongue got sore on both sides today. But I am going to carry on with **not** using the mouthwash as that seems to be helping a wee bit, with the sore gums. My tummy seems to be working better already.

24th February 2024: I was saying about people being negative but when it is a real thing, they need to talk and **all** will be real things.

My knees were sore in the night that is from the cold, I think. I have had sore hips and/or knees for many years, when cold, especially in bed. It is a beautiful morning this morning.

One of the reasons I find, "don't worry about it," so annoying is that it is like saying stop talking about that, it is **not** important at all. It is like they are taking it, your thoughts and feelings away from you. I realise that it is actually said because people are caring about and trying to look after you, but I have always found it really annoying and was just thinking about why that is. I often reply to Dad (in good times before all this), "I'm not worrying, I'm wondering".

25th February 2024:

(See Video Diaries on *See Salt Tears* Website 25th February 2024)

I am still sleeping so much better. I woke early morning but again I was so much calmer and relaxed than I have been. I have realised that one of the differences is that I am not repeating things, ideas, worries and thoughts over and over in my head for hours. It was important for me to note that all down, which I tried not to do, but needed to. It was luckily getting a bit light by then, so I didn't have to put the lamp on, and just wrote the word "Repeat" down in big writing, twice. That did the trick, and I got back to sleep until it was time to get up.

My nose has still got blood in the gunk in the mornings. The bad rash, on my hand, is getting better but it seems to have moved to my face which is looking very blotchy. I have a sore tongue and knees, my lower legs still feel heavy, and my feet have been feeling a bit numb at times. These are just some of the effects that are still happening but most definitely moving in the right direction with this healing, already.

I have, for many years, drunk a lot of water but the Dr Who Regeneration seemed to make me very dehydrated. I am still having to drink a lot more than before. I would say 3 or more times as much.

This evening, listening to my CD's I found out that I can nod my head to the music now, without feeling yucky.

26th February 2024: The burn was coming up in the night. I nearly took a tablet but decided that there won't be so much chemo in it, so it shouldn't do so much damage. I managed to get back to sleep fine. I was also, very farty, so I know that is a good sign that my tummy is beginning to work better.

It was a lovely day and walk round. The glaziers are coming today.

I am waiting for glaziers. I am a bit stressed with the not knowing when they will be here. I usually would be, at the unknown, but it is worse today. I am uncomfortable in my side and sleepy. But am better now as I have just decided to forget about it and get on with my things. It is still more than usual but I am getting on better.

Oh, they arrived just as I was typing up the notes for this. Lovely, and I have just left them in peace to get on with the work. They are no bother at all. It is funny, strange and interesting just how much stress can be caused waiting and wondering for something unknown, that is really not a problem at all. It **doesn't** help to know that, at the time of the stress. It just shows that it is not the thing, but the unknown that is the problem.

I was looking at the new houses (there are loads of new houses being built in our wee town) and the old D & D Dairies building, which is obviously going to soon be knocked down, and the land made into yet more houses. I thought about how I should take photos of these things. It is a part of our history. These are things that I don't think of taking photos of. As I write this book, it becomes history. It is an important record of society and one individual's experience. I should explain more about things that are going on and not just assume people will know. Also, it is a part of culture. A small town in rural Scotland, is very different even to other places in Scotland, never mind other places in the world.

I have always been different, **not** in with fashion or trends. But as I get older, I am very out of touch with other generations, especially a lot of the younger world. I realise, that is nothing new and it has been like that forever, also that I was young, and that I still am considered young, by many.

For the glaziers coming, I cleared away the rest of the stones and shells but forgot about having no or little eyelashes. Now my eyes are all gritty feeling. Hopefully my eyebrows will grow back soon enough. It will be interesting to see how long that takes.

(I have a collection of stones, shells etc on the window ledges from many years of adventures and gathering interesting things that catch my eye when out and about.)

I was just looking at the medicine bag that I have kept in the kitchen over the time of my Dr Who Regeneration. It is very strange and wonderful not to have to take any medicine anymore.

I don't know what has happened tonight, but my eyes are so tired, I am having to stop reading my book and go to sleep earlier. I am burpy and uncomfortable in my left side and have the taste of tablets in my mouth. Perhaps it was the dust or stress earlier from the glaziers, but I don't think so. I think it is because I used the computer too much today. This is the way that I used to feel when still working or when I wanted to try and fix the hard drive or work something out and used the computer too much. That made me feel like this, **not** too much, as it was still much less than I did before Dr Who Regeneration. Hopefully that is all it is, and I can get a good sleep. Also, because Dr Who is finished now, that I will be able to use the computer more and more without getting this. It will be interesting to see.

27th February 2024: I was awake about an hour from 4am but was fine and relaxed. I have heavy lower legs. The Thai chi instructor, when I used to go there years ago, always said that it was a sign of being fit and healthy, when you could get out the bath without using your hands or arms to lift yourself up. That is hard for me to do, just now, but I still can and do (very carefully).

My face is bad with blotches today, I look like I have some rash type of illness. The wound from the operation marker is a bit yellow and red around it. I think it is okay though. I will wait until Thursday and see how I am. This is Tuesday.

I am feeling good this afternoon. I have tired eyes; I might have to think of something to do that is not on the computer.

28th February 2024: I woke up to some saliva in my mouth. I have never noticed not having that, but it must have been like that for a long time. Hopefully, that will be the start of my mouth healing up.

I had a lovely lunch with Helen and Dolores.

I was awake from about 3 or 4 am. I had bad burning. I used the big cushion for a while, which did the trick. I don't want to use the medicine if I don't need it, as it causes or can cause constipation, and I am doing so well. I slept well, was relaxed and waking up from dreams which I wasn't having, or not aware of, during Dr Who.

29th February 2024: There was less blood in my nose gunk this morning.

I was a bit lethargic for my walk, today, but got on and soon went further. I had a lovely walk.

I have carried on with my yellow sheets for these two weeks after the Dr Who finished. (The filling out, with numbers, how you are doing in the areas that they ask about, for the treatment). It is called a diary but is really, just a tick box sheet. That is the card finished now. So, I think that I will stop doing that. It has been interesting to keep the record. I will see how I can use the data. Perhaps I could make up a graph, somehow.

It will be strange not to fill it in now. It was really meant for the staff and for checking each week how I was doing, although it was all done verbally. It was handy for me to have in front of me, especially, when my head wasn't working right.

March 2024

1st March 2024: I had to laugh, I realised that the toilet was bubbly as I had put washing up liquid in the cistern, to clean it, and that it was nothing to do with my health or wees!

4th March 2024: Today, I am starting the Art2Life, free art workshop, that I was telling you about. I was awake a lot from 5am, Friday night and Saturday morning, worrying about it being a scam. But it seems really good. There have been three days of ½ hour chat videos. The actual thing starts today or really, tomorrow, because of the time difference. I am looking forward to doing this and seeing what happens to my art and life.

7th March 2024: I am looking forward to my art class today. I am putting off going on the computer yet as that is what seems to make me really tired. I had a nice walk round. I just talked to Dad on the phone, and I still get extremely stressed at the tiniest thing. I was asking how Sue and Mairi had got on at the hospital. I think that the art class is maybe a bit much for me, but I am loving it, so am going to carry on. I am burpy and a bit tasting tablets now that I am off the phone.

My autism is still so much more emphasised. I am uncomfortable in my side. Dealing with people is still really difficult. It is fascinating and I feel, very important, that it is all so much more or bad, at the moment.

8th March 2024: My first day of no blood in my nose gunk. I am numb, a bit, in my hands and feet, my arms in the night and my legs in the day. I need to move about more, later in the day.

10th March 2024: It is interesting and really weird, that the right sides of both of my legs appear to have little hair now, but the left sides are still hairy!

I had a lovely day and walk. I had a lovely time with Dad and Duncan yesterday. We went for lunch at Delivino's. I am doing good although my legs are still numb, at times.

I finished my art course week. It was not a con, just a massive marketing thing. But I really enjoyed it, and it **was** free.

My nose just dribbles down, still, with no warning.

13th March 2024: For the last few weeks I have been feeling like I have a wet back. I have realised that it is clothes on my skin with no hairs on my back. I am not a yeti!! It must just be, that the downy hair is now all gone.

I have a very runny nose in the day. It just runs out nonstop in large amounts. I am not needing Vicks vapour rub. It happened when writing this. I just leaned forward. There are no hairs to stop it and maybe the top of my nose is not blocked now?

14th March 2024: I thought that my nose was unblocked but I woke up in the night from a terrible loud noise, coming from my nose. It is a roaring sound like someone making a really loud, bad noise on a brass instrument.

I think that I am going a bit daft. I lost, a while back, my wee black crystal. I probably just dropped it but, yesterday, I have lost the letter that I wrote to my friend Ruth. I went up to the bank, Abdul's and the COOP and it is not there. I have also lost the bee coin that Graham gave me. I have no idea where I have put it.

I just put on my clothes and the coin fell from the heaven's! So that is great.

I am feeling good and so much better, generally. My tummy is working well. My nails are so much better. You can still see the yellow, lined parts, but they are moving, up the way, now only on the top half of the nails.

I have had a twitch, in my lower left eye, for the last three days.

15th March 2024: I thought that I better be brave and sensible enough to go and ask about the lump on my thigh, before I go for my operation on Wednesday. I phoned the staff in Perth, and they said to go to the Doctor. I went and she thinks it is just the tendon that I am feeling, and that it is the same on the other side. I am not sure that I believe her, but I am very relieved and happy about it.

Hilariously and embarrassingly, I was so happy when she said it was fine, that I slapped my thigh! She must have thought, what is she doing. I tell her my thigh is sore and then slap it! I did it again when sitting back on the seat. I also said, "you would tell me wouldn't you", when she told me that it was not a lump. What a daft thing for me to say!

17th March 2024:

(See Video Diaries on *See Salt Tears* Website 17th March 2024)

18th March 2024: It is interesting, I have been stressed and feeling a bit down and tired today. Loads of lovely people have been wishing me well for the operation but that and packing my bag, made it all real. But I have just been reading the Fern Brady book and thinking about and finding out more about her autism, has helped me think more, about mine. That has taken my mind off the operation. So, I am going to take a bundle of paper to write on in the hospital, if I feel like it.

Today I am thinking that I might have symptoms like diabetes. I read, the other day, how that can be caused by the steroids. I am tired, blurry eyes, dry mouth, lots of wees in the night etc. But all much worse today and sore. I looked at my notes about the Fern Brady Book. It is interesting to read and find out more, about her autism. (I am burpy, farty and my side is uncomfortable.)

My nose is blocked and runny and I am hot. My knees and shoulder are sore. Is it just all the chemo coming back, because I am stressed? It said that diabetes can be brought on by stress. My back, face etc are getting itchy again. The writing is flying out of me, again. Is it all to do with my autism? It is obviously the chemo again and what I am going through, but also really interesting.

The doctor asked how my mental state was, when she phoned, a few months ago. I just replied that I was doing good but that I knew that bad days are allowed. That is what Babs told me someone had told her. I don't think that I can think quickly nor know what to say when asked. My old boss had it right and brilliant when she would sit quiet and wait for me to eventually speak. I would come out of those reviews, shaking, but she had got me to say what I needed to say, which helped us both. That was long before any mention of me going for the "Aspergers" tests. She was a brilliant boss and person. More people should know and see that.

Maybe writing is my new therapy. It gets my thoughts and ideas out, which I never get to do, as I can't or don't communicate, in the ways that people usually do.

I have a headache, and both thumbs are working away. I don't want to have this paper and pen by my bed, tonight, as I have to get up at 6 am on Wednesday morning, so, I want to sleep well tonight.

The hairs appear to be slightly growing back on my left forearm. I only noticed, as it felt rough, the right arm is still smooth. I looked in the magnifying mirror and a couple of wee white hairs are growing back on my chin! I don't ever want to pluck them, after having lost them all, but I expect that I will soon forget about that idea! That's fair cheered me up and made me smile. ☺

I was reading Fern Brady talking about when plans are changed for a night out. She says she is an adult; she had no way to explain her behaviour. I really liked that. I know so well, when able to think about it, that my behaviour is odd and feel bad about it. So, reading it here, makes me feel better. It is a real autistic thing and not just something that I can just switch off because it is odd, or weird, or not adult.

She was talking about how all the stuff online is for parents with autistic children, not for adults with autism. I am noticing that so much, at the moment, with all the pages, articles, online magazines etc.

She also, earlier in her book, talks about how people always say, oh everyone is a wee bit autistic. That is so much what happened to me and about, you don't look or seem autistic. I suspect that this is so much more so for some older autistic females.

She mentions not being able to do eye contact that day, when in a bad state. I am noticing that so much at the moment, at the doctors, in the shop, talking to the neighbours. I realised, after being at the doctors, that I had no idea what she looked like! She wore a jump suit thing, but I don't know what she looked like. I also saw and talked to her about the lovely tree picture that she had on the wall.

It is interesting when Fern Brady mentions how her therapist told her that walking can really help with autism in that the repetition of it can be helpful. I never knew that. I absolutely love my walks. Maybe I should find out what kind of therapist that lady was and see if it is possible to go to one. Not something I would choose or want to do but it might be interesting to find out more. Books are so brilliant, every one of them can help me to learn and find out more, so much more than documentaries etc. Especially, or particularly, books about actual people's lives, written by themselves.

She talks, again, about how, if she is overloaded, she will stop making eye contact. I have noticed that so much more these last months. I thought it was just me noticing it more but maybe it is more than that. More at the moment, with what I am going through. It is all just too much and no one, including myself, knows that it is to do with the autism. It is like the cancer is a real thing but "Asperger's", not autism, doesn't show, so they and I forget about it or don't believe it.

19th March 2024: I have been doing so much better generally.

I sat outside this afternoon. I did a bit of weeding with the hoe. I got quite a bit round the garden before I had to stop as I felt it in my chest. It was lovely to be out in the fresh air before the hospital and operation tomorrow. It is going to be a right nuisance with the sun this year. I love the sun but even in the cold out there today I felt it a lot. I will have to wear my cap and suncream a lot. Never mind, that is not much to have to put up with. It must be so annoying for people with bald heads having to wear hats in the warm sun.

I had a bit of a panic in the night but got to sleep. I am very tired this morning but had a lovely walk round the park and am feeling quite calm again. I am all packed for the hospital now. I only have to stay in one night. Then I will go to Dad and Sue's and see how I am doing after that. I tried to fit everything in my wee backpack that I take on my walks but decided that was silly so got the bigger bag. It always feels daft how much I take to things, but actually, I haven't taken very much at all.

20th March 2024: That is me in the hospital. I got here about 7.50 for 8 am. Everyone is lovely. There have been lots of questions, some repeated. I am tired and it is scary but hunky dory.

I am in my gown thing, which you put on back to front, with my dressing gown and surgical stockings on. There are two other patients and another one just going to be arriving soon as they took her bed out.

There is a lovely big window across the room with a great view of a bit of Perth and the hills beyond. It is a grey and rainy day out there.

I don't really want to start talking to the others as then I will have to keep talking. I keep forgetting that I have a baldy heed.

I am sitting down as they were mopping the floor, and I don't want to start a conversation. I would like to just stand and look out of the window. I don't want to sit too long as I will be lying down later and not so bouncy then!

I am feeling daft standing, but I want to keep active. I went to the window but there is a lady having a personal conversation with the nurse, so I came back to my place.

It is **10.05 am**, I expected that it would be a long day. I would love to go a walk.

I haven't written any notes about the operation time as obviously I was not in a position to be writing notes! So, I will try and write a bit about what I remember (it is now 9 months later as I am typing this up).

I was told to get into the bed and then wheeled along the corridors, through the hospital and down, in the lift, to the operating theatre area. It was very strange and a bit scary to get wheeled along, while lying in the bed not knowing what was going to happen nor how it was going to go.

I was "parked" in the waiting bit in the operating area. That was a bit sad and scary. There were a couple of staff passing, who said a wee hello to me, and one had a wee chat to me. I saw someone getting wheeled out of the operating theatre area and, later, another patient, in their bed, getting brought in. One of the staff said that I had been brought down a bit early. I lay there and tried to relax.

Eventually they arrived and started telling me what would happen. They wheeled me through the doors and into a wee room. There were three of them, I think. One was a student, I think, as they were getting told about things that were happening. They did checks, connected me up to things etc. Then I was given the mask to put me to sleep. I don't think that it took very long to work.

Next, I knew, someone was calling my name, and I was crying. I think it took a wee while for them to wake me up. I was fine and in the recovery room. I then got taken back up to the ward.

643 pm: I am doing fine. I have been sleepy. They had to put the cannula on the underside of my left arm, so I have to remember not to knock it.

Sue phoned to see how I was, about 5.05 pm, so they asked me and let her know.

I have got up to the loo for the second time, fine, so I am allowed to go myself now.

There is only one other lady patient now and she has had a bad time so is sleeping.

They said that my operation went fine and that they only took one lymph node out, which is great. I have got up to get my book and this paper to write on. I was waiting until it was dark, while I could still see out the window but thought that it was time to sit up more and do something, before I get too sleepy. It is quite dark out there now.

I think that I maybe stayed in the recovery area for a while. I will have to ask them about that, if I remember.

I don't know if it is the lady's machine or her phone that is making a beep, but I am sure they will be watching and keeping an eye on it all.

I thought that I had taken blank paper but there is a Christmas list on the page!

I am looking at the beautiful, coloured butterflies on my new Kindle cover.

I think that it is the lady's monitor that is beeping every wee while. Hopefully I will forget about it soon. It is lovely, peaceful and quiet generally at the moment. I can hear the men and nurses talking in the other rooms.

My lips are very dry, but my mouth is fine. I don't want to drink too much, in case I keep having to get up in the night. I am doing fine with my right arm. It is my left hand, with the cannula, that is a bit funny, but I have wiggled it, and it is fine. I feel a bit daft as there are so many people about that are a million times worse than me. I just heard my name. I think they sometimes think that I don't have a cannula on as it is on the underside.

I think that I will have a wee read of my Kindle now and see how I get on with that.

8.45 pm: The lady's machine was not plugged in, so that was what the beeping was. There is a man in the other room who, I think, gets a bit muddled but is quiet, mostly.

I heard the oyster catchers flying past. It is lovely to hear them. I am glad that I know what they are now, from home.

My left hand is a bit numb but not bad.

I have bruises on my left arm, like when we used to do the "Hootchie Choochtie" dancing (That was our fun name for, Scottish Country dancing. When we were getting whirled round, our partners hand would grab the top of our arm to whirl past. The next day the top of our arms would be covered in purple, finger mark, bruises. We did Scottish country dancing at school, parties, barn dances and weddings. I wasn't that keen on it at school but am so glad that they drummed it into our heads, now, as I still know how to do the dances when at weddings).

I wonder if I am just meant to get up and go and do my teeth and things or wait for them to say? I reckon that I will wait an hour or so. I didn't get up to get my chewing gum (I have, for many years, taken chewing gum after eating a meal so that my sensitive gums don't get sore, later, when I brush my teeth.) earlier but I got up to get the red mini brush tooth thing for my wisdom tooth. (I have a sideways growing wisdom tooth that makes a hole against my other teeth which I can't get the toothbrush into.)

I read my Kindle for a chapter. I couldn't work out how to turn the page, as it doesn't have a button like my old Kindle did but the other lady said that it would be swipe and it was. I kept dozing before I finished the page and rereading the same bit then I must have been dozing as it switched off a bit. But I worked out how to get it back on!

It is getting a bit chillier now. I will stop writing soon and put my arm back under the cover. I need the loo again. I will try to stop drinking now. One of the staff just filled my water jug up.

9.50 pm: The nurse said that it was fine to put my nightie on, so I have brushed my teeth, had a wee bit of a wash and put my nightie on. That will be better now. I still have my pants on. Maybe I don't need them now that I have taken off the operation gown, but I will leave them on just now and see if they drive me mad or if I will forget about them. I will read a wee bit now of my Psychic Art book and then go to sleep. That man's buzzer is going again. Oh, it has stopped now.

21st March 2024: I didn't sleep much at all but had a good rest. I am allowed home today. I should have been home yesterday.

The nurse wanted to check my wounds before I left the hospital. She looked at it and said did they tell you it would look like that. I hadn't looked at it yet, so I looked down and said, "No, it has never been that big in my life!". As my boob was all swollen from the operation. The nurse laughed, she had meant the colour, it was all green from the dye that they used. We both roared with laughter.

22nd March 2024: I have had a great day at Dad and Sue's. Yesterday, I was putting my earrings back in (I had to take all jewellery off for the operation) and dropped one down the loo! Poor Dad and Sue heard a horrible screech and thought that there was something terribly wrong. I wanted Dad to get the earing out so quickly, as I didn't want any germs. I am still so used to not being allowed to get any infections from the treatment and now after the operation.

In the hospital, I thought that I was not to have a bath for ages, but I was delighted to hear that I am allowed baths. They just have to be shallow and to keep the dressing dry, for ten days. I am not to use deodorant on the right side. The nurse said that I, "won't be stinking, we make far too much of things like that", she was right. ☺

25th March 2024: It is so much better than my operation back in 2011, when I had my monster cyst. Yesterday I was getting a bit sore and uncomfortable, using the mouse, but I am much better today. The exercises that they have given me to do are going really well.

I arrived back to the flat Saturday afternoon (it is now Monday) and I am doing very good generally. I am not that sore and am sleeping well. But I am very tired. I tried to go back to sleep this morning and get a long lie, but I gave up by 9am and just got up. I think I am very mentally tired more than physically.

I was getting more and more upset. I didn't know who to talk to or what to do. I wanted to go my walk but couldn't go out as I was crying and did not want people to see. I thought about going to the Health Centre and asking to talk to someone but thought that I would have to make an appointment and didn't want to do that.

In the end I phoned Dad and Sue. Dad came and got me. I had a good talk with Sue, then had my lunch with Dad and walked home afterwards. I am very tired and will have to stop using the computer soon, but I wanted to write this down as it is very important.

I am not sure what my notes were saying here but it was about autism and Dr Who Regeneration, I am very tired even when I have slept, now added to that is the new thing of me using up a lot of energy to heal up. But I hadn't slept before, so I am even more tired now.

I just can't cope with making appointments or arrangements. I know all the answers I know what might happen, I know I can cope with it etc. I just need someone to talk to and tell everything to, not to fix it but just to listen and understand.

My autism is so much worse when I am like this and all through this. That is a thing that people can't see or understand at the best of times. I am very scared about everything; I still care about and think about everyone. I can't be in control of things yet; I need to know what is happening as I can't settle when I don't. My nephew, Jack, will be here this weekend, but I don't know what is happening at all. I have said that I will just be up at Dad's, on the Saturday, but can't sort it out, get times etc. I know it does not matter at all but that does not help. This is a thing about autism that people just don't understand. I know the answers, I know the sense, but that does not change the feelings or stress. It is a million times worse when I am tired, stressed, ill etc. I am getting too tired to type this, I will have to go off the computer now.

Sue asked, about the Jack weekend, she said that Dad is talking to Karen (Jack's mum), so, could I not, just not think about it, for a few days. I just need to let someone else worry about things and deal with them. My autism doesn't work like that. I know all the sensible answers, what I should do, what I should leave for others, but autism is real and irrational. Mind you, it did help, her saying that to me. I am not used to outside advice and wisdom. Maybe that would help but with a lot of over and over, every time reminding and repetition. So that it became rote and a part of me. It is the thinking and processing that can't be done or not so much, depending on the state of stress.

I am lucky to have had only a couple of panic attacks in my life. Today was one of them. I couldn't breathe or was breathing and panting. It helped actually. I haven't been able to breathe properly for a few days when trying to say something to Dad at all stressful, or changing anything. It is the first time, in **all of this**, that I have cried in front of someone.

I have been wondering what would have helped most and it would be to have someone ask me and help me to work it all out and through for myself. So, I will try and remember that for others, rather than giving advice. I will try to listen and ask.

I am here on the couch and having a wee snooze which I never do in the day as I want to be able to sleep at night.

I was a bit cold and feeling sorry for myself. Then thinking how I am lying in a central heated flat and am so lucky. There are **so many** people a million times worse off. But then I realised, that is not what this book is about. It is about this journey and, also, being on the autistic spectrum. I can be brave, we all can, but that is not going to give you any info or insight into the journey.

So, I will be a different kind of brave, one that will help me in a therapeutic, cathartic, positive kind of way and, also, help you and others think about, process, sort out and understand more about their own or others journey in life.

(I was trying to get the word cathartic there. I had put lethargic and knew that was **not** the correct word. I got Google and Ai to help me but was searching for a word that started with L! I finally got it from Ai, who had kept suggesting, "liberating", when I realised that it might not start with an L. I also began to think that it might be something like carcinogenic! Ai got if for me when I changed my question and asked: "what is the word that means helpful in a getting it out of your system kind of way, something like lethargic, cleaning out". There you go, a great example of what my brain has to go through when I know a word but can't get it!)

The sound in The Chase (tv programme) was sounding wonky today. I have a sore mouth and side, I have the mouth ulcer ridge, both of which I thought were because of the Dr Who but perhaps they are just from being in a strange state and very tired.

It's confusing, with autism, occasionally I need to talk to someone but mostly and even then, I can get on better on my own.

31st March 2024: Okay, so a very private thing and not something that I would usually discuss with anyone, never mind the whole world in a book! But doing this may help others in similar situations. I had to take the dressings off tonight. It was very scary. I did it. There is a raggedy, very thin line where they took the lymph node out. There is the same kind of thing but in a ring right around the nipple (areola) area It looks like they have made a big circle round it and opened me up there, for the operation? They did say that there is glue over the wounds, so maybe that is what I am seeing or maybe it is dried blood from the wounds? All going out from the circle, are puckered lines. I will have to see how it goes after time and once it has cleaned up a bit and had time for the dressing marks, dye etc to go. I am all dye as they had to tell how things were flowing and what they needed to remove.

The nipple looks a bit strange and flat. It is all quite weird, strange and scary but basically it is still a boob and still much the same as the other one. If a bit wider and flatter looking. I expect it is still swollen and that will change too. They said that I could go to them and get the dressing off if I wanted to but that it was easy enough to do. So, I chose to do it myself. Perhaps it might have been nicer to go to them, purely for emotional support and being able to ask questions.

(Update: It has healed up really well. I didn't like the idea of the big circle round, but it is a really good way to do it and much better than another line scar.)

Anyway, it is done now, and the best news is that I can have my proper baths again now! I do love my baths. They are my therapy. I was so happy to hear that I was still allowed them all these last 10 days, but now I can have lovely deep baths and lie back in them again.

I am doing very well. I still can't cope with any badness, at all, and get very stressed with people, if any change or anything at all, really.

I am very tired after a lovely weekend. I was at Dad's yesterday, then Delivino's for my nephew's 30th birthday. We were in Comrie (a local town) today and Glenturret (a local whisky distillery) this morning.

Last week I had a panic and big cry on Monday and a big cry, in the night, later in the week.

I also noticed that my eyebrows were a dark line, they are suddenly coming back. This morning the bottom of my eyelashes have suddenly appeared. The hairs are also coming back on my chinny chin chin!

We went a walk to see the Earthquake house in Comrie. I have never been there before. It is an interesting wee place. My tummy was a bit bad, and I was very farty which I don't suppose is the best thing at a place that records earthquakes!

April 2024

3rd April 2024: There has been changes or additions of words or phrases recently, such as, "raw" honey and "wild" swimming and camping. I know the reason why; it is not that which bothers me. I don't like change, but it is the change of sound in the pattern, it jars me, and I know that it is not right. I find that interesting about how my brain processes things. Dad says "folk", for people, recently which he never used to and that does the same thing.

Another example of how my brain processes things, in a game we were playing, the answer was Serena Williams. Dad got me to the name Sienna; I could **not** get the answer, but I knew that that name was wrong.

4th April 2024: It was a great day today. Dad took me to Dundee to get my results from the surgeon.

I was taken into the room, and he asked how I was doing. I replied that I was doing good but that I was very scared about this. He said not to be scared as it was good news. The lump, which has now been removed, was down to 3mm. There was no sign of any other cancer around the area and none in the lymph node. So, it is all so brilliant.

I now just have to heal and then get the radiotherapy.

He also examined my wounds and she, the lady helping, and the surgeon both said they were looking great.

So, a very good and positive day.

I still can't cope with any bad. It is all very scary and tiring. It is brilliant to be able to tell everyone the good news but also very scary. I don't like to relax or get too comfortable or raise people's hopes. It, the cancer, grew in the first place and could do so again. I think people need to work out exactly why it grew. My eye is twitchy, and my tummy and ribs are tight. I don't want to write this as it seems so negative after the great news. I nearly stopped and nearly scored it out but the point of all this, is to tell it like it is, for me, **not** what I think people want to hear. It is also a big effort to tell so many people and have to "talk" to them all (well message them). (I say so many people, but it is hardly any, really. Just my brothers and my very close friends. I am so lucky to have them. They are wonderful. I am just trying to explain how I feel inside as it is important for this book.) Everyone has their own things, and I am just so tired still. I am also worried about the radiotherapy.

But it is, all, wonderful.

I hope I can sleep well tonight after all the excitement. I am sleeping so much better now. I am also very lucky to be getting left alone in peace and quiet so I can take things slowly and start to heal up.

When I let Diane know today, she said that she was so looking forward to hearing all about it, from my own point of view, in my book. I loved that and really appreciated it. I don't know if this book will work. It is so full of negative thoughts and feelings. No one wants to read depressing things. But I reckon it will. It will be worth it, and my good sense of fun and humour will shine through.

As I say to Dad, it is really important to not mind about getting praise or waiting for other people to like something.

Just write the book for yourself. That is what is so therapeutic and doing that, in turn, will help others and the feelings, thoughts, bravery, life and magic will, doing that, shine through from this roller coaster of a journey. It will be interesting and help others along the way.

Dad was asking today if I had told any of the professionals about my not being able to cope with any bad or stress at all. I answered, no, not really, as I had found out that brilliant and lovely as they all are, they just have time for the job that they are meant to be doing. But that I would write about it in my book although that would only be a tiny bit of it. People can't see what is going on inside, so, it is really important to try, even if only a bit, to let them see and understand. That is not something any of us really do, much, but I reckon that it would help society thrive, if we could and did.

Dad said it was a bit like we can see that you have lost your hair and things, but we can't see the other things. That is what autism can be like too and why it is so important to listen and find out so much more about it all.

Later on, after the excitement of the day and the good news, I got into one of my thumbs going, can't relax or switch off, states.

My eyes are twitchy, my thumbs are going. Everyone has their own things. Everyone is being so lovely and patient with me. They all care so much. Many people are so much worse, but it is not about less, more or whatever. All I can do is focus on me and write this. It is helping me so much, getting all this out. If I just do this and write the book, then afterwards I can see if it is suitable to let people see. I reckon that it will be like when the magic happens in art, photograph, computers, and sitting out in nature. When I get lost in the world of something and just get on with it. Stop thinking about it. Enter another state. That is when the magic happens. That is when it is good and when the light shines through and out. That is what we should all do. Find our magic and do it.

See Salt Tears

I am so tired. I have been lying here, with the light off, trying to relax and switch off for about ½ an hour. Thinking that I should put the lamp on and write as it would get it all out of my system but also thinking it would be better not to and to get to sleep. But the longer I do that and the more I think about it, the more buzzing I get. It is all too much excitement. In good times I have learnt to avoid things that make me like this, too late in the day, so that I can switch off and relax. But these are not normal times, at all.

My throat has gone that strange way when I try to swallow and clear it but is kind of hot and sore the way I do that. I feel it in my ears and my left side is uncomfortable. My thumbs are dancing.

I am worried about Dad, this is all so much stress for him, over all these months. He has been so lovely, patient and understanding. My nephew has started telling me things again, which is lovely that he trusts me, but I just can't think about anything but myself just now. I couldn't cope with the news on tv. I only watch the 6pm news but it is too much. So bad and negative. Why can't they tell positive, motivating stories? There must be so much news that would and could help us, get us to hope, feel and be positive. News that would motivate and give us hope to get us to believe and know that we can do things, sort things, be things.

My eyes are so heavy, my nose is burning my lips are tingling, my mouth has that medicine taste. I don't want to put the light out now as I think I will just have more to say. More to get out of my system. Burning is coming up a bit, I am burpy, my boob is sore from the operation. I am buzzing.

Still, it is so much better than when I was having the Dr Who Regeneration. Now I can stop, I can sleep, I can switch off. I need to try and get to sleep now, to calm down, relax, think, meditate, ask questions in my head, go on a journey. It will all work now. I can do it.

I have found out, over the past years, that if I have a pain then I can go into it (in my thoughts) and that can help it go away. It is as if my body is trying to tell me something and by "going into" the area of pain, I am listening and paying attention to my body. So, that really helps. I am doing that to help my sore boob now.

So, what if I could try going into the buzzing? Would that help? That is more difficult. I will have to work out what it is I am feeling so that I can go into it. I was making a noise, so maybe I could try going into that.?

My eye is twitching again. It is time to try this new idea and to switch off.

6th April 2024: I am doing so much better. My feet are still a bit numb, but I walked up to Dad's much better. I am still a bit slow but quicker than I have been. I even managed the steep hill of King Street without being too sore in the chest or out of breath.

Dad and I played the Bemused, Befuddled and Bewildered board game. We call it the "old people's game". I got a bit stressed at times and avoided the charades that were anything like the word "fall" etc. But I kept calm, and we had a great game. My eyes are getting better too. I was able to read the cards without the magnifying glass.

I am still tired, but it is a good tired and I slept well last night. I am managing to stay up until, nearly, my old time, before going for my bath.

My head is a bit itchy tonight, like it was when I first started losing my hair, but I am hoping that it is a growing hair itch this time! I am getting some dark patches showing vaguely over the white. It feels lovely and although it does not look curly, like they said it might be, I can feel at least one curly bit, at the back and the top. It is fascinating to see what it might grow back like.

I currently have two tufts of hair above each ear, too short to lie flat behind the ears. Which makes me look like a goblin or elven character! I am trying to think what creature or being it reminds me of. Someone from one of those films or fantasy series but I can't think who it is.

(I have worked it out, with the help of Google Pictures, who I am looking like, it is Grandpa from the Munsters! (The Munsters, 1964))

7th April 2024:

(See Video Diaries on *See Salt Tears* Website 7th April 2024)

10th April 2024:

I am doing good, still really tired. I wanted to go back to sleep but wanted to get up. I think that I should just go back to sleep one of these days, and soon, to heal me up, before the Radiotherapy. I think it is a bit like the healing needed after a trauma. It has been months and now I am just healing up, so the reaction is coming out. Dad always said I was great in a crisis. I am very calm but then, afterwards, I am all shaky and upset.

I want to talk or rather answer things on the internet, take my Scrabble shot etc but I am just so tired. I feel it like it is too much, in my chest. It is really strange being well but not being well. Two days ago, I went out and did a bit of gardening. It was lovely and good for me to do it, but I was so surprised how I had to stop. I felt it in my chest (physically different from the stress feeling that I talked about) I had to stop and sit on the chair and read my Asterix book. I love doing that, but it is so weird to be well and yet find that I can't do things.

I am too tired to use the computer much, so I am just writing notes, for this. It feels stressful, as I feel time is running out before the radiotherapy and also then, healing time before going back to work. I know that is daft and that I have plenty time and that there is no rush, or hurry for anything, but remember, sense doesn't really help or work with this nor with autistic stress. It is all very fascinating, I feel it physically, in my chest, eyes and I am so tired, my mouth is dry. It is a bit like a panic attack but just a gentle one, if you could get a gentle one of them!

I wrote an entry for a competition about Hope where we were to choose 3 photos and write no more than 250 words to go with each photo. I was pleased with what I did and was going to re-read it then enter it today. Then found out it was for EU citizens which I thought I was but realised that I am not, as they mean people from the EU that now live in the UK. So, I can't use the entry. I then realised that I had saved another writing competition thing to do and that it was called Hope too. So, I thought that I could send what I had done, to them instead. But then realised that it would be put on the internet, and I have not announced on Facebook or to many people about what I have been going through and it would be put on very soon. Not a thing I feel comfortable about doing yet or in that way. Well, I liked what I wrote for the entry, so I am going to paste it here. You know what I have been through now, as you are reading this book, so no worries in that department!

Stories of Hope

Journeys

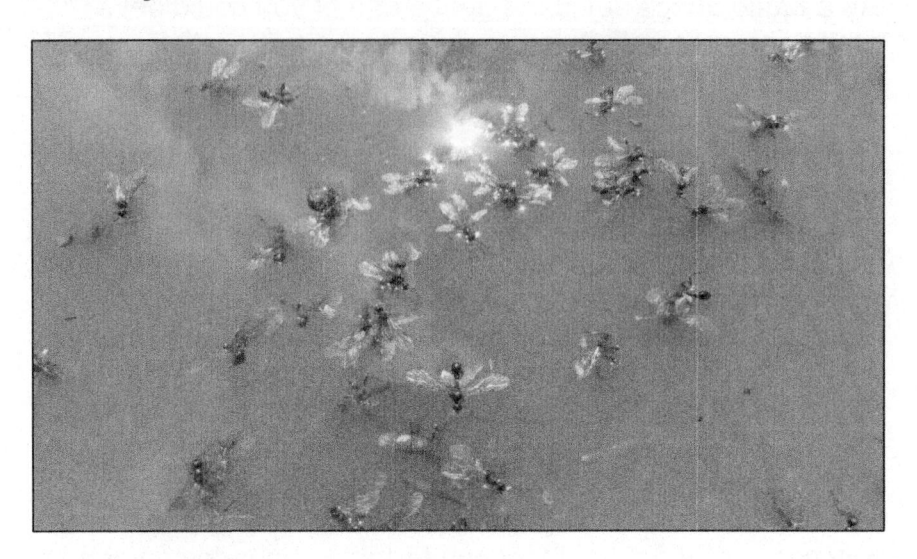

Life and Death are the two things that happen to us all, no matter who we are.

I have been on a long journey for the past year. Not one I would ever have chosen but one I have moved through.

I saw this incredibly interesting but sad sight on a walk in August. The ants were all dying in the large puddles. I helped some of them out, but apparently it is just part of our natural world cycles. The larger queen ant, starts her life with wings, then, on "flying ant day" the male ants grow wings. They fly away from their nests to mate, which they do in the air. The male ants die soon afterwards.

I didn't use this picture in my photo page as it was just too upsetting, but I also find it very beautiful in a strange kind of way.

My Hope is that we all learn to love and respect ourselves, leading on to us all, then, loving and respecting everything, everyone and this magical world on which we live.

Identity

I am currently in the process of writing my third book. *See Salt Tears* is what I plan to call it. It will tell the story of the journey that I have been going through, for the last year, finding out that I have breast cancer, the treatment, thoughts and feelings. All seen through my eyes within the autistic spectrum.

It is strange for me to write this down here knowing that it will go online. It is not a story that I have yet told many people, and I am not one to talk about my personal things. Writing out my thoughts is so much easier for me than talking about things.

My first book, *Living* Diagnosis, explores how I experience the world and society in a different way from many others. My second book, *Answers Inside Out*, carries on from that and tells how creating, writing and thinking about my first book, led to me finding out and getting an official diagnosis, at the age of 51, that I was on the Autistic Spectrum.

My hope is that being brave enough to write our own stories will help others and that all society can learn and grow from each other's experiences.

Aspirations

I am an author, artist and photographer. I absolutely love to be out and about in our beautiful world of nature.

All the seasons are beautiful and have their own magic and wonders. However, I wait all year to see one of my favourite treats, butterflies. Then I wait for a sunny still Scottish day, not always the easiest thing to find! Off I go to find and see these beauties.

This photo was taken in September 2023. At that time, during treatment, I was very tired and could not manage to walk far. My Dad dropped me off and I made my way along a short track, living and enjoying our magical world of nature.

This peacock butterfly was just one of the many showing off their stunning colours and patterns among the flowers that day.

My hope is that I can show people the beauty and magic of this incredible world that we live in.

It is amazing what an incredible tool we have now, in typing, where the computer marks all the spelling and grammar mistakes and possibilities. I am aware that Ai would even write things for me now but what is the point of that? What is the point of getting it to do art either? Well, I know it is to save time and get what you need, like a tool, so you can spend more time on doing things that you want to do, but for me it is the creative part that I love, so that way of doing things is not for me.

Oh, this is great I am doing so much better now. This has really cheered and woken me up. It is really like I can't deal with other people as they change my path and journey. It is, I think, really an autistic, um I am trying to think of the right word . . . like expansion, it is so much more. It is like I can usually cope or what they like to say, "mask" my autism much more, but now it is so out of my control. I am in a state like I am distant and looking out of a narrow gap from somewhere, further away. I can do fine and am very happy and relaxed but even the thought of having anything to do with others, such as looking at messages etc, makes me feel in that tight chested, tired state again. It is all very fascinating.

I realise that I am repeating things and thoughts over and over but that, in itself, is really important. This is real, this is happening, and I don't think that many people will have written such things down, in such detail, nor as they are happening. I always think that I will remember about things but there are so many things, details that we forget, in even a few days or hours, about events and what happened. I know that there was feedback in a review of my last book saying that "the writing is sometimes rambling, sometimes pedantic", but then it goes on to add, "but, as such, it provides a unique insight into the thought processes, concerns, and "different" view of life of someone with Asperger's". I love this as it gets the point.

That last book, which the reviewer was talking about, was written when I was completely well and *compos mentis*. Now the thoughts are flying, and the rambling is part of my every day and night head or rather normal being. The getting them out or the writing of this, is such good therapy and one of the best "medicines" that I have found. All it needs is for one person to read it, shine a torch on something, and pull out the important, magic and life changing part that will help in some way to unravel part of what we all go through as we carry on and move through our personal life journeys. As I have a picture head, I will try to explain what I mean by this with or rather illustrate the way that my head thinks about or sees this and what I am trying to get through. Bear with me, it is rather a long and elaborate, winding story for an "illustration"!

I am currently playing a computer game called, "Magic the Gathering." I really love it. It is a card collecting game that I used to play with my wee brothers, years ago, where they collected the cards.

In the computer version, you can get an animated pet who sits beside your cards as you are playing the game. Mine is a green dragon which I love as I love dragons. Anyway, one of the recent "pets" that people have been getting is a mole. This mole, when you click the mouse on it, shines a torch back and forth in front of it. That is what is needed, here, in my writing, to find the magic and find the gems. If you are the kind of person who likes to cut through the chaff!

It also makes me picture the blackbird or crows in the garden when they are in my cauldron planter and trying to find tasty bites to eat. They peck through and rapidly throw out, to the side and behind them, all the things that are in the way and not tasty, like my very lovely rainbow abalone shell. The shell does not like being thrown out, onto the ground, very much, but the bird does not really care. It needs to get the food, moss or whatever it is searching for, to carry on with its lifecycle and journey.

Well now, I will probably have completely lost you, but that is me so much better and brighter. This is my head working like it does and that was all an illustration of just what goes through, this particular person's, autistic, picture head, while thinking about something.

10th April 2024:

I wonder if the book should just be called, *Lumps*?!

I have been watching Fern Brady as one of the guests on the *Great Bake Off* (a tv programme where contestants have baking challenges to get through). Which, after reading her book, is very interesting. I wonder what I would have thought of her if I hadn't read her book or known about her autism.

They said, in the programme, which was a charity show, for cancer, that everyone in the world is affected by cancer. That made me wonder if the people in tribal groups, far away from others, have it too?

The hairs on my face are growing back, they are sticking out like a white hedgehog! I need to wait until they grow a bit to lie down, I think.

11th April 2024: I am doing really good today. I have been out in the garden doing some weeding. I stopped, sensibly, as I was getting a wee bit tired and am, now, enjoying sitting in the sun and reading my book. There is enough cloud to hopefully, along with my cap, stop me getting too sunburnt. It is still a very cold, wild wind. I have got the suncream down to use but think that I will have to go and get my coat instead! It is going to be a strange summer having to think about suncream much more with no hair. It is well on its way back though. The very white is beginning to get a bit of dark grey on top, in patches. It looks a bit like mould when I see it in the mirror sometimes! It is lovely to be sitting out. The sparrows are chirping away and now that some of the neighbours washing has been taken in, I can see some of the birds hopping about searching for tasty bits and pieces. Oh, something is going on. I think that was the starlings getting very upset there. All is fine again. Right, I will go and get my coat. I still have a balance of a cold neck, from no hair and too hot. I've no idea how bald men put up with thinking about all these things all the time. They must get roasting having to wear their hats all the time.

I was having a good chat with the new neighbour earlier. She seems really nice and a nice family too. It looks like it is going to rain now. I will go and get my coat and stay out for a bit more.

I am going up and down the stairs to the flat so much easier again too. It is lovely to be getting well again.

Please excuse all this yo-yoing back and forth. It is all part of the journey and so I hope you will understand that it is important to this book. I see that I have to get a new sick note at the beginning of May. This is only the beginning of, or not far into April, but I am looking at the calendar and see that there are only 2 weeks to go until I have to think about what will happen next. It seems like it would be best if the radiotherapy would hurry up and yet I do not want it to, at all. I am just needing to rest and heal. My side is getting uncomfortable, my mouth is dry, I am tired.

I will have to ask for a chat with the doctor, I think, to see what will happen with the next sick note. I have to find out when my 6 months off work will be up. I want to get back to work, to help Diane but the very thought of even one day working at the computer is so tiring, never mind 3 days and dealing with even the nicest of people or even slight stress, is far too much for me to even think about.

I can't see how I am going to be right. And that is without the radiotherapy. How is that going to make me feel? Even without the stress of having to work out how I am going to get to Dundee every day. Oh dear, now I have a bit of a headache, and my knee is sore! Oh, I was doing so well. Isn't it daft, it is all just maybe and what ifs. Also, we are all under threat of losing our jobs once again. I have been able to switch off from that and forget about it, but, I think, that it is this month that we are to hear. Oh well, I can just have trust and faith. Now, I will just be happy and get on. I am away back to read my brilliant and magic, special edition, hardback copy of *Lord of the Rings*.

I have bits of songs and sayings that I say, a lot, to myself for different situations. Now I am singing, in my head, "it will be all alright, we'll have a drink on a Friday night, it will be oh so good, we'll do everything that I know we should." It is, I think, words from a single (record), that I had as a teenager. I have different memories of chunks of words from songs, adverts etc, that I say to fit certain things. That, I think, must be an autistic thing. It is not something that I think about or am aware of. It is just a part of me.

I have a clock, a small round black one, which is really an alarm clock, that sits on the centre of the small fire mantel piece that is in my bedroom. The wardrobe, at right angles to it, has a full-length mirror on it. At times, I look at the clock, in the mirror and watch the second hand go round. Only, it is magic because, of course, in the mirror, time goes backwards! My stress is whiled away.

14th April 2024:

(See Video Diaries on *See Salt Tears* Website 14th April 2024)

I was trying to get and print out timetables for the bus from PRI (Perth Royal Infirmary) to Ninewells (Dundee Hospital), yesterday on Dad's computer. It took ages. I was getting stressed but did fine. I got there. I was stressing out at the time that it will take, **every day**, to get there, wait for the next bus, get back etc. But I got on with the board game, *Dingbats*, with Dad.

Suddenly, in my head, I just decided to be happy, have trust, I know all this, and I will just, let it be. A very, wise Beatles song, "*Let it Be*".

Today the sun is shining through the closed curtains. I am going on the River Earn Walk, I think. I will look for the kingfisher, the cuckoo flowers are out. Maybe there was too much rain yesterday, but maybe I will see butterflies. I will watch the river and live and feel the magic.

15th April 2024: Autism is such a strange thing, it doesn't go away just because you can be sensible, and your head can tell you not to make a fuss. In fact, trying to do that, just seems to make it all feel ten times worse.

I have an appointment with the oncologist tomorrow in Dundee. I was just going to switch off the computer tonight and go for my bath, when I saw, on Facebook, an alert saying that there would be major hold ups in Perth tomorrow, for roadworks. I know that Dad likes to go through Perth on route to Dundee. So, I phoned him to tell him. He said that we should go the other way and would have to leave a bit earlier. We agreed on 1.50 instead of 2 pm. The appointment is at 3.30 pm.

That was all that happened, but I got all stressed and more stressed as I was trying not to make Dad stressed! Now, everything is fine, but I have phoned back, three times! All to stop stress and causing, I expect a lot more stress. Now, I am later for my relax and reading my book time. My thumbs were going, and my tummy is tight, my mouth dry. All for something that is perfectly fine. Also stressing out poor Dad, when he is not so confident now in driving to Dundee. He stays so calm, patient, and lovely for me with all this. I was doing so well. It is really, very fascinating, the stress levels that all this is causing and how much more severe it makes the autism. Mind you this is **all** far from normal times.

Knowing that I am stressing my dad out and that I shouldn't, really doesn't help at all. In fact, it makes it so much worse as I try not to do that, and that seems to be the worst thing to do.

16th April 2024: I had a great day today. I went my walk round the park, this morning, it was a lovely day. The butterflies will soon be out.

I went to Dundee for the appointment with the oncologist. He says that all is good. It will be about 5 to 6 weeks before the radiotherapy starts as there is a waiting list. I will have to go in before that, so that they can scan and work out where the machine is to work. It has to be in exactly the same place each time. You get given three wee dot tattoos, so that they know exactly where to place me and the machine.

The great news Is that it is only for nine days. I was thinking that it could be up to a month of travelling to Dundee every day. So, nine days is so much better and such a relief. It is five days of radiotherapy and then four days of extra, on the exact place where the lump was.

That is me signed off from the oncologist now. I chose not to take the stuff that goes into your bones. That was a choice I could have had but he was fine when I said that I didn't want that unless it was really necessary.

Now it is time to sleep, heal and recover.

It is fascinating how many people don't recognise me, such as a lady this morning, whom I was at school with. I always thought that it was daft when famous people wore sunglasses etc as a disguise but maybe it really does work. It is interesting to see how people act. That lady smiled then looked away, she did not look back when I said, "hiya." I realised that must be how she would act to a stranger. I was at school with her and have said hello to her for decades.

19th April 2024: I'm doing good. I went for a walk around the park this morning. I have started wearing my cap instead of my woolly hat as it is getting warmer. The cap is a bit itchy. Sometimes I am brave enough to take it off to itch my head. Soon, I may be brave enough to go without a hat. I am just waiting until two wee patches that still look a bit bald, look better. But I will have to wear a cap for the sun, I think.

I went for lunch with Helen and Dolores. We tried the coffee shop that I used to work in, many decades ago. I didn't feel like Delivinos this time and they always laugh as I always choose there, so I thought that I would choose somewhere different. It is a nice place as it has a good, old fashioned, antique shop on the floor above the café.

I went up to the till, with Dolores, to order my own lunch. I ordered my sandwich and drink but when I got back to the table, I realised that I had forgotten the soup. So, I went back up to the till to add the soup to my order. The lady asked if I wanted crisps, which I had asked for with my sandwich, or soup. I couldn't think. I wanted both. I must have taken a wee while as she said she would just put both. I went back to the table and was upset. I was crying. It is amazing as just the slightest thing can upset me. I really can't deal with people yet.

There was no reason to cry. I felt embarrassed thinking about it later, but it is real. The lady who served us was at the table later and was a lovely lady with a lovely smile.

I was sucking the ice cubes at the end of my drink. That shows just how much better my mouth is. I couldn't have done that a few months ago.

Now I am going out to sit in the garden and read the Prince Harry book. I am really enjoying it. It is really interesting, so far. I also love to take a Tin Tin and an Asterix book down. I love them and it really relaxes me to sit and read them. They are fun. I collect them. I will soon have them all, especially the Tin Tin books. I see that they are making some new Asterix books. I am so lucky to have a garden that I can go and sit out in. I love the fresh air, nature and the birds busy chirping and singing away.

I am feeling a bit sad today for some reason. But am happy, well and contented as well. I read a work email today that says we will find out, next week, about what jobs are going. I have been through that too many times now. I have always survived, so far! Well not really, as my full-time job went from five days to two, then, later, up to three. Let's hope that I can carry on with the job. I do love it. Maybe I just need to have trust and faith. Anyway, whatever happens, I am an author, artist and photographer.

Right, I am in the middle of watching a film. I am enjoying it. It is called "*Mrs. Palfrey at The Claremontt*". But it made me think of this book, so I wanted to write it down. I will get back to my film now.

22nd April 2024: I was awake and roasting quite a lot in the night. My thumbs were going. Perhaps it is from reading Prince Harry's book? It conjures up deep feelings as he was talking a lot about his mum.

I was going to go back to sleep this morning. I still haven't had a good long lie yet. I woke at 8.15 am and went to the loo. I tried to get back to sleep, after that, but had to get up at 8.30 as I needed a poo (I know you don't need to know that!)! So, I just got up and have done fine all day. It has been a beautiful day. I sat in the garden this afternoon. I put the fountain out for the year. (It is a large planter thing that we put a small solar power pump in, and I have some wee coloured glass things in it.) I just got a small amount of water in the bucket to fill the fountain up and did two trips. I thought about it for a while first. It is lovely to see it working again. I thought that it would be broken after being in frozen solid water before it was put away last year.

I saw three butterflies. I might go a picnic walk tomorrow. It is to be nice. I will look for butterflies while the cuckoo flowers are still out.

I met a pigeon on my walk this morning. It was being attacked by a big crow and a sparrow was there too. They took off as I walked along. The poor pigeon's head was all damaged and bloody on the ground. I was confused when I heard something moving. I looked back to see that the noise was coming from where the pigeon was. Watching, I realised that it was still alive and trying to get back upright. It was moving round. I stood over it, then nudged it, gently, with my foot. It was definitely still alive. I hesitated and looked about, not knowing what to do. I have avoided any bugs, dirt etc, for months, as I can't fight infections or couldn't. But I decided that I had to try and help it.

I gently lifted it up, in my hands, so it was sitting up the right way. I then looked at the road, pavement etc, where could I put it? A lady came along with a dog and said to the dog, "keep on, keep on". I thought of leaving the pigeon under the shade and shelter of a parked car but decided that the garden would be safer. I walked a wee bit up the drive of one of the very large houses and placed it gently in the plants under the shade of a small tree or bush. I then left.

I should have given it a bit of healing before I left but I went on. I don't know if it could survive but it felt so gentle just sitting there in my hands. I know the other birds needed food for their lives and families, but I am glad that I helped the pigeon.

23rd April 2024:

(See Video Diaries on *See Salt Tears* Website 23rd April 2024)

A wonderful day today. I went a walk by the river looking for butterflies.

We are to get an email from work tomorrow about yet again losing jobs. I got back to an email from my boss. He has asked for a meeting with me tomorrow morning and it is with the HR lady. Oh no, I really can't even think about this! My side is sore, and I feel a bit dizzy. Never mind, life is a journey and what will be will be.

May 2024

1st May 2024: I am doing good. I had a great sleep for the first time since early last week after hearing about us losing our jobs.

I wrote a letter to the doctor. She was going to give me two more months, from now, for my sick leave, but I explained about my full pay ending on the 10th of June. So, we decided to make it until then. I don't know when the radiotherapy is going to start but a month away doesn't seem like a lot of time to heal up, even without having that. But I can use the holidays, that I still have to take, to help out as and when needed.

I have been working on a video with my views about losing my job. It is very tiring for me to use the computer a lot, but I do love a project like this, and it will help me to get back into the swing of using the computer, before I get back to work. Also, it is really important and healing for me to get it all out of my head. Although it causes me a lot of anxiety and stress worrying if anyone will like it, if it is stupid, who will see it, how can they see it? If I put it on Facebook, then people would find out about my cancer and I haven't told them yet, if it would upset people, if it would get me into trouble, if it is daft etc, etc, etc. It, the video, was 50 minutes long. I have managed to cut it down to 15 minutes. People just seem to like short, snappy things of a couple of minutes just now but, well, I reckon that it is worth it.

I am very tired. My nose feels like there is liquid in it again, my side is uncomfortable, and I have a headache but just as I am writing this. I am doing good and am doing the right and write thing! Getting all this out of my system.

I am happy, peaceful and calm.

2nd May 2024: This morning I went to have my bath only to find a monster had moved in! Here is the poem that I wrote for that monster:

Today there's a monster in the bath.
In the night I feel you laugh,
tickle, dust and catch my feet.
You eat and rid of beasties neat.
Incredible creations you weave and sew.
Hiding high, lurking low.
You scuttle forth along the floor.
My fear and nature make me roar!
Please excuse me, human just,
out the window, go you must.
Feast for birds? Watch that crow.
Thank you, Sir, now off you go!

I love doing cryptic crosswords or trying to. I was just trying to work out a clue:

"The normal way of digesting any cranial meat left (10,5)"

Look away if you want to work it out for yourself!

I thought it might be an anagram. I like anagrams. I worked out what the answer was and, like always, I checked at the back of the book to see if I was correct, before writing it into the grid.

I said the answer out loud: Sedimentary canal then looked it up. I knew the answer from the anagram and the clue before it, but this is a perfect example of when I get words a bit wrong! The answer was, as I knew, alimentary canal.

3rd May 2024: I got my pre-radiotherapy scan today. It went hunky dory. It was a lovely, bright waiting room with large, high windows and hanging, giant rectangles, like wind chimes that caught the light. The staff were lovely. It is just a circular machine. (I wasn't sure what to expect when looking at the pictures and leaflet about it.) It is not very comfy to put my arms up and back, but I did fine. I got the three wee tattoos, they are tiny. One on my boob, one under and one on my left side. The picture in the leaflet, of the tattoos, must have been zoomed in as it looked like the marks would be bigger.

I got my dates. It is to be from the 27th of May to the 6th of June. It is a bit bad timing as I have to go back to work just the week after that. But I can use up my holidays if I need to. The times were bad, one too early and most around 4 or 5 pm. They very nicely changed some of them for me. Now there are only 3 or 4 late ones. I will take my tea to eat, like a picnic in the car. I have a gown, to take home, which I am to take to wear for each of the radiotherapy sessions.

I went for lunch with Dad and got some time to sit in the garden this afternoon. I am very tired tonight.

4th May 2024: I am so tired. I woke up from a dream where I was at a job interview. A lot had happened, I think, already in the dream but I was at a table, with the interviewer lady, to my right, round the table and Dad to my left.

She had been turning over cards with pictures, a bit like tarot, and I had begun telling her what I thought about them. We had got to a bit where I had to read a large paragraph problem and tell her what should have been done. I couldn't read, nor concentrate. I tried, she gave me time and went away. Dad was talking and I said that I had to read it. He tried to explain that it was fine, but I was not able to think. I couldn't read and had to get on with it, but the "wall" was down.

Being stressed is like that, so, I will write this here, it is connected with my head not working. That 'state' is much worse than anything I have ever had but it is also from my autism and not being able to read when people are waiting. So, I use my finger to follow the writing and read it out loud, but it still might not work when there is a large amount of text to be processed.

Then, back in the dream, Duncan came along, talked to Dad and put his big green waxed coat on the interviewer's chair. That is when I woke up.

Perhaps this is the **start** of me healing on a mental level, as well as a physical one. Also, I am very tired and a bit worried about going back to work. This is also all muddled in with the threat of losing my job.

I have been thinking so much, this morning, about my work, autism, change, working from home etc.

Thinking of cancer and how we can get through it. Anyone can get cancer. However, I feel that it helps, to get through the treatment, if you are already a fit, healthy, happy person, if your body is not already damaged by various addictions. smoking, drinking too much, eating too much of the wrong things etc. However, that is very general and not always the case. My mum was a young, fit, healthy, happy person but didn't get through it. Also, there are many people with addictions who live to a great, happy, old age.

I suppose it would help to understand an addiction. Even if you are able to get through long enough to feel better, see the difference, manage, understand that you don't need it. It all changes when "it" is dangled back in front of you again. It is a massive cycle. But like the trauma cycle we can do it; we can get through and change.

We can do it. We can do anything. We can get through cancer. We watch these people on the news going through unimaginable traumas and tragedies and they carry on. Why? Because that is all they can do.

We can get through death, even deal with our own. There are two things that we can be sure of in life. One, that we are born, the other, that we die. What happens in between and how we deal with it is up to us, in our own heads (no matter what).

All the way through this journey, my book was going to be called, "Lumps that go Bump in the Night"", but after writing the notes about that, I decided to call it, "No Matter What". This then changed, all in the same thoughts, to, "See Salt Tears". That was the one that felt right and that is what it is.

5th May 2024:

(See Video Diaries on *See Salt Tears* Website 5th May 2024)

6th May 2024: My first day out, without my hat, today. I don't mind how it looks as it has grown back to just look like very short hair now. In fact, I quite like it. But it made my tummy feel a bit funny as I didn't want to talk to people about it.

I went a walk with Babs round the park. I soon forgot about not having my hat on. She was just leaving me to go home while I went to the COOP (supermarket) when I suddenly remembered about not having my hat on. It was fine. My hair is looking nice, just very short.

7th May 2024: The oncologist phoned this morning. They can't tell from the scan where the lump was, so can't give me the boost radiation to that area. So, I don't get the second week of four days. I just get the first week of five days of radiotherapy. I suppose that is not good for the chances of stopping the cancer coming back. But it is brilliant, in that, I only have five days of the treatment. Also great in it meaning four days less of travelling to Dundee.

I finished and sent Diane the link to my video in response to losing our jobs. It is 30 minutes long! (I must have been wrong when I thought that I had cut it down to 15 mins!) It is very scary to let people see it and wonder what they will think. Diane really liked it and sent me an email to say that, but the email got lost. The one before and the one after arrived, but not that one. So, I was wondering.

8th May 2024: I was awake from 3am for an hour or two, thinking about the video that I have made in response to us losing our jobs. I had a lot to think about. My thumbs were going.

I've had a good day. I cut a bit of the grass today and managed fine. I felt it a bit, in my chest, at the bits that were too long. I was very sensible and only did the two smaller areas then stopped. I have left the large, drying green bit for another time. I then sat in the garden and read a book.

I am so happy to have got the grass done. I have not been doing cleaning or gardening. It is all too much, and it has been piling up. It is really lovely to be doing so much better.

This morning, I walked through a cobweb in the kitchen. I am reading my lovely massive, illustrated *Lord of the Rings* book just now. I never usually read a book more than once, but it was many decades ago that I read it. I am really enjoying it and am surprised that I don't remember much about it at all. One bit I did remember was the bit about the giant spider. That must have really bothered me. I didn't get the same feeling from it this time and noticed lots of other bits about that whole scene this time. However, walking through the cobwebs is still not my favourite thing to do! I don't like spiders as they lurk and then disappear or scuttle across the floor, then disappear behind or under something and I don't like that feeling. I do love them when I am out my walks though. I also realise that they are wonderful things to have in your house as they eat the beasties.

9th May 2024: I am tired after my walk today. Now, I am not wearing my hat. Two people stopped me to talk. One asked if I had been getting a new hairdo and the other said that she did not recognise me with my short hair. Both said they had not seen me for ages. It is funny how people are recognising me again now.

It was a bit much to talk and also tiring, to stand for a while to talk. I can walk fine but find standing a bit tiring. My feet are still numb. The first person was talking all about cancer. It is not that I can't cope with or say that word it is just that I don't want to think about it. In a way I think that it still just makes it too real for me. It was a good story he told me, as he had thought that he had cancer, but it turned out that he didn't.

The other person was asking if I had been in hospital when I said that it had been a long year. It was a bit of a strange conversation, I think, as I never actually told her what had been wrong. It is funny but I just seem to expect that people should know. She just kept looking at me, questioningly. I just said that I was doing much better and was now back out to annoy the world again. After she had gone, I realised that my voice had been getting louder and louder. I think I maybe do that when nervous or stressed?

I then had to stand in the supermarket queue for a long time while a man bought what looked like 50 million lottery tickets! I still leave a good, "Covid", gap between myself and the next person in the queue but everyone else seems to have forgotten about that. I reckon I love that gap much more, as it gives me space.

When I got home there was a message from the health centre saying that there was a sick note waiting for me. It is really funny, as I got the sick note after talking to the doctor, the other week. Then I got in from the garden yesterday and there was a message that there was a note waiting for me at the health centre. So, I went down, and it turned out that it was the same sick note. They must have asked for one for me when the doctor got back from holiday, not knowing that she had already given me one. Then today, there was the message that there was a sick note for me! So, this time I just phoned. It turns out that it was the same thing again. Weird!

I then got a phone call from the radiotherapy people in Dundee. The lady was saying that I could get some of the appointment times changed, if I liked. So, I have got the three days that were around 5pm changed to much earlier in the day. Which is brilliant and so much better as we would not have got home until after 6 in the evening with the old times. That has made me much more settled.

14th May 2024: I talked to Diane and sent the video to the lady in the college who is a union member. I have still not heard back from my "boss boss", who I also sent it too. I have a fizzy lip, tired, dry mouth, acid reflux etc, probably from the stress of talking about the job losses and sending my video (yes, I am feeling it in my chest again just typing this).

So, I put the computer off. I finally got the hoovering done. I felt it a bit, in my chest, but did fine and now it is all done and looking lovely,

19th May 2024:

I was just thinking how nice that it is, being able to think again!

My hair is growing back in nicely. The wee tufts above my ears look a bit funny though. I love it. I smile every time I look in the mirror and see my new swirly white hair, looking back at me.

It must still look quite strange though, as I was walking along a path today when a man and wee boy came cycling along towards me. I went to one side of the path to let them pass. I could hear that the man started to say to the wee boy, "move to one side to let that lady past" but he only got as far as the "l" in lady and stopped, then mumbled. The closer he got; he wasn't quite sure what I was!

20th May 3024: I have just finished watching a series called, *Dinosaur,* on BBC iPlayer. It is a comedy about the life of an autistic woman dealing with the changes on the lead up to her sister's wedding. I really enjoyed it. It was a wee bit slow, to start with, but I soon got into it. The characters are all very caricatured but then it is a comedy.

One of the things that I noticed about the main character, Nina, was when she was stressed and trying to cope or help by rubbing her thumb and finger together. It was obviously emphasized for the filming, but it is so what I do with my thumbs and when I hold my hands together.

This morning, I was on my walk round. I noticed as I walked past Aldi (a supermarket) and then B&M (a large shop) that I was holding my hands together and twisting them tighter. I have been thinking about and noticing when I am doing that more, recently, because of having watched that programme. But this morning I was thinking about it and realised that it might be because of patterns.

I can see patterns or rather I see things and notice something that is different or not right, in the big picture that I see. It stands out to me. When I started my hand rubbing, I noticed that things were getting busier, not just people, but cars, lorries, things going on. I reckon that it is too much change all at once, to the pattern that I can see. Maybe that is why I, and some other autistic people, don't like lots of busyness and things happening all at once. It is too much to process and focus on, all at once. I then can't sort out or process everything that is making the pattern different.

I have been tired, had a dry mouth and a bit achy today. Oh, an orange tip butterfly just flew up to me and then away. How lovely. I have come out to the garden. I was going to get the laptop out and start typing some of this up, but I felt I needed a break from the computer. The garden is such a lovely healing, fresh air place.

It is a great sign that I am thinking about work, autism and patterns and things again. I was just saying to someone, I met this morning, that I can think again. It is so wonderful to be well again.

I feel like I want to write but I don't know what to say. I think this book, or the notes for it, is nearly finished. I will still let you know how I get on next week with the radiotherapy. Then I have going back to work along with the stress and horribleness of the job losses. I know things happen for a reason and I just have to deal with what comes along. It is so much easier to know that and do that, when feeling better and not so tired. However, it is also good and healthy to think things out, to work out how you feel. I have found that writing is a great way for me to do and deal with that.

I just have to remember to listen to my body and take a break, to change the scene and step away, if I can, at least for a while. Right, it is time to go back up to the flat and see what time it is. I think it is time to make my tea. Yes, I was just writing to a lovely work colleague today, that I do still have my times for things and no, I don't want to change that. And yes, it does make me happy. It is one of the ways that I look after myself. Structure is yet another pattern, I suspect.

25th May 2024: This is Saturday. On Tuesday and Wednesday night, I was awake a lot. I was **very** tired by Thursday. I think it is partly the heat and also, subconsciously, I am very stressed about the radiotherapy week and the job losses. I have had a dry mouth in the evenings and fizzy lips. I am happy and cheery though and doing really good. I had a scary, red eye today. I am so tired that I could sleep for a million years and that is **before** the treatment next week.

It is rather terrifying that it (the cancer) can come back but it is still absolutely brilliant that there is only the one week left to get through. Then that will be me completed the journey.

I have done the hoovering, and I cut the grass, the other week, but nothing else like dusting or the cutting the hedges. I wanted to get it all done, before next week, but I haven't, and I realise that it is not important.

I am just going to rest now and look after myself. I am so tired, with using the computer, the last couple of days. I can't imagine going back to work, but I know that I will just have to use up my holidays. I realised, this evening, that I am looking forward to going back to work. I don't want to lose my job but if it happens, then that will just be my next journey into the unknown.

I got the most lovely reply from my bosses' boss about my video. It was a couple of weeks after I sent it. It is a very personal thing, the video, I don't suppose many others will see it, but I just have to have trust and faith. What will be will be.

I am really enjoying the challenge game that my brother, Calum, gave me. Dad and I play it each Saturday.

27th May 2024: Well, that is me up fine, at 7.45 am. Dad is coming for me at 8.45. I have made out a table with the times for each day. The time to leave, time to arrive (ten minutes before the appointment) and the time of the appointment.

Today is the first day of Radiotherapy. I have been to the loo, and it is 5 minutes before the time to leave. I don't like to be late, and Dad will be waiting there for me already. I will get a wee bit of fresh air as I go out.

I am in the car now. I don't want to be rude to Dad and I can't get my head into writing. It is obviously a different part of my brain. This is making my side uncomfortable as Dad is trying hard to be quiet. My mouth has gone dry, and I just wanted to write this bit. Now, I will stop writing and spend the lovely time with Dad.

"Quiet is not a bad thing, when I'm driving, but I do enjoy your gabby chat!" I loved this. A great quote by Dad when I said that I am not going to write but I might be a bit quiet.

10.05 to 1028 am: I am out of the treatment, amazingly quickly. I thought that I had just left Dad 5 minutes ago.

The machine is very like a spaceship. It is so weird, nothing at all to feel, but doing all that to you. There was a lovely picture of green trees on the ceiling. There was also a cross in the ceiling where the machine or whatever, works through, when I shut my eyes, I could see the cross. They said that the machine was doing some x-rays first, so when they came back into the room, I couldn't believe that was all the treatment done, I thought it was just the x-rays.

They must have very good eyes to see the tiny tattoos. It was uncomfy having my arms back, but fine. My left arm was uncomfy but fine. It is funny it is the left arm that is sore and not the right one, where my operation side was. The bed is **not** comfy.

Dad says that the ladies in the waiting room, the last time, said that it was after a day and half that it suddenly hits you. Let's see. I am very lucky it is only going to be for five days.

I am home now. We went to Tesco's on the way home. I am feeling very tired and a bit fed up, I don't really know why, as it can't be the treatment already. It feels a bit like people just think that I should be fine as there is nothing to see and nothing bad. But I am doing good. I have been a wee walk round. Do you know, I think that I might just be feeling a bit funny as I have been in the car, and also it is thundery, heavy and hot.

That's amazing, fascinating and terrifying, it felt like the machine hadn't done anything. As they said you don't feel anything. But tonight, already, it is all hot and red all around the treatment area.

28th May 3024: I am doing fine this morning. I have a sore left shoulder. I was awake a few times, in the night, but opened the window wide and listened to the morning chorus, from the birds. I mostly had a great sleep.

Sue is taking me today. Graham tomorrow and Dad, Thursday and Friday,

I am delighted to be allowed my baths, I phoned and checked as I forgot to ask yesterday.

I was thinking, the other night, how incredible dreams are. Everyone can dream, even if they don't remember. Yet many don't believe and are extremely suspicious of psychic, spiritual, etc things. We say it is because we can't see them, they are not physical. If we can see, feel and be inside a whole different world, every time we go to sleep, then it seems that is a massive area that we accept but don't think about how incredible it is.

I was out of the treatment and back at the car in about 20 minutes. I told the ladies that I was tired and a bit achy. They said that was fine. I think they may have been a bit wondering about the red around the areola where my operation was. It is red and a bit puffy which is what happens with the radiotherapy, so I don't suppose anything unusual. But I got the feeling that they were checking it. They talked quietly and after the treatment had started, they came back in and checked again. They didn't move me at all. Perhaps it was just a check of the machine or something, but I wonder. Anyway, I didn't ask.

I am doing much better this afternoon. We were back in Crieff before 12. I went a walk round and managed up the steep hill fine, yesterday I couldn't be bothered with it.

I think that I better get off the computer now as my eyes are very tired. It is time to make my tea anyway.

29th May 2024: Graham took me today. All went fine. I had an appointment with the nurse after the treatment. She said a lot of the things from the leaflets just to make sure I knew about it all. She said it might give me a inflamed lung, and oesophagus. She said I might get a dry cough. I have a sore throat a bit tonight but that may be from the car journey and talking.

My left shoulder is still sore at times. It is very uncomfortable, after lying on the bed for treatment, with my arms back, but not too bad.

I was awake quite a lot in the night, but I think it is just being unsettled from this week. It is still a much more relaxed awake than it was before with Dr Who. I didn't have to leave until 1.45 pm today, so got to take my time in the morning and sat out in the garden for a bit of fresh air before the journey, which was really nice and relaxing.

30th May 2024: I had a nice time with Dad today. It took a wee bit longer again; it must just be the early appointments that you can get taken early. Not long though, just about 30 minutes.

It was a different side of the area, staff and room today. It didn't have the lovely trees on the ceiling. Just the same though. It went fine.

Dad and I went for lunch on the way home. When I was coming back to the car, I suddenly went really tired. I then got absolutely roasting in the car. I am just feeling tired now but fine.

I was obviously totally wrong about the second day when I thought they were checking my boob as it was all red and swollen around the aureole. They just put me in the machine then go out the room to check things, then come back in and check things again. They do that every day. So, I was making things up the other day and it just shows how I shouldn't!

I have had a sore throat yesterday evening and just now, but I reckon it will just be what the nurse was saying about yesterday, things getting inflamed from treatment.

Only one more day to go.

31st May 2024: Finished. Yaba Daba Doo. 😃☀️🗣️🦉🐾🦋

I am very tired. But it is so wonderful to have finished this journey. Like all journeys it has taught me lots and made me think about many things. Thank you for your help and company along the path. My writing this book has helped me so much and hopefully it will help you and others in turn.

I nearly handed in my t-shirt and went home with the hospital tunic!

June and July 2024

2nd June 2024:

(See Video Diaries on *See Salt Tears* Website 2nd June 2024)

I am doing good. I had a wonderful walk and sit down by the river.

Yesterday, playing Calum's escape game, I got stressed, a dry mouth etc. But I had great fun. I don't know if I am ready to start work next week. I might just do the Tuesday, then take holidays. I am very tired.

I was thinking that I was going to have to get Dad to get me home today when I was walking down. I had really tired legs and felt numb. But I did fine and got back fine.

I am still having to drink a lot of water in the evenings.

5th June 2024: I am sore round my eyes. I have bad, dry skin. Strangely, the loud, roaring, snoring noise, seems to have moved down to the back of my throat instead of my nose tonight.

8th June 2024: I am doing good, just tired still. I saw, at the end of a video that the Crieff museum had put on

Facebook, that they have put some more of my photos up. So, I went in to have a look. They have also put up the bit of text about me, with my photo. That is wonderful.

I was talking to the lady there about the photos. She looked at the bit about me and said, "yes, what happened to your hairdo?" I answered that I had been ill for a year, and this was it just growing back in. We then went on to discuss how it is coming back with a wave which is nice.

It is strange, I just assume that people will see my hair and realise what I have been through, but, obviously, they don't all work that out.

I love my new hair though. It makes me smile each time I look in the mirror. I also love it out of my eyes.

Sometimes, while writing my notes for this book, I have thought that I can't keep writing all these things which might sound negative, moaning etc. But I have realised, as I have gone on, that it is a good, positive, therapeutic thing to write this journey down and show and explain how it went and just some of what it has felt like.

Oh, my goodness, I am so tired tonight. I have spent the last ½ hour trying to read my book, with my eyes shutting and me jolting awake again. Well, they said that the effects of the radiotherapy would peak, 7 to 10 days after the finish of the treatment. It is now, 7 or 8 days, depending on how you count it. Now it is time for sleep.

9th June 2024: I worked out that, for me, it is boring in a book and film, when they tell me what to do. It is okay to tell my story as I can move along, experience and think about the journey. While writing down my thoughts, feelings and ideas. Then make my own mind up about things.

Oh, my goodness, I could sleep for a million years. On Tuesday, I go back to work! Today, I have had a wonderful, peaceful (in the human department), magical walk and picnic sitting down by the river.

I don't know if I will stay back at work, even if I get to? I have a whole plan for B's World (my website, now called See Salt Tears). Maybe you will be able to enter it already as you are reading this.

The video diaries on the website have a slow pace, **not t**he trend. It is not about marketing nor making money, but it is magic, so I reckon that is my next "project". I better get this book written and finished first.

10th June 2024: Back to work tomorrow. I am still very tired but doing good. I felt strangely fed up and sad this morning. I went a walk to our lovely park. I will miss my longer walks round, that I have been doing each day. I sat in the park and had a good old talk with myself, in my head, don't worry! I was nearly crying. I thought and sorted through things. I ended up smiling and thought, right, it is time to get on now and carried on my walk home.

It said, in the info, that we might get a bit down and depressed after the treatment finished, as we were no longer being looked after when we have been getting so much attention and care over a long time. It is brilliant to be well again. It is funny to think that all the illness has actually come from the treatment. I know it is the treatment that keeps us alive though.

Well, I am off to go and plant my tomato plant into its bigger pot. I even managed to go to the shop, down the road, buy and carry back a big bag of compost. I reckon that is a sign that I really am getting back to normal.

I know this is nothing to do with this book and have been doing my best to keep on track with the theme of the book as I go along making my notes. But I just want to tell you about my tomato plant as it is moving on and growing things, which is a good, positive and a great step forward.

Sue makes us crackers each Christmas. This Christmas the jokes that she put in them were help the world jokes. We were to rip them up and plant them! So, I did. I also planted my tomatoes in a small pot next to the cracker surprise plants. I had them sitting in the stairwell. After a while they started to grow but a load of wee mushrooms also started to appear, all over the soil. I thought I better remove the mushrooms. So, I did, and changed the compost as I thought it must be old wet compost that was causing the trouble. Unfortunately, the plants were too young to survive the change. All my tomato plants died and only one plant, from the cracker surprise plant pot, kept on growing.

The other day I was seeing that the plant was getting big. I presumed it must be a flower, but it was going to be a big flower. I also had a bit of a suspicion that it looked like a tomato plant! So, I sent a photo of it to my sister-in-law who can tell what things are by using her phone to identify them. I said not to spoil the surprise but just to let me know if I should put it in a bigger pot. She answered that the bad news was that it looked like none of my cracker flowers had survived and the good news was, that I was very good at identifying tomatoes! It is indeed a tomato plant!

So now I have a lovely tomato plant when I thought that they had all died and I am off to plant it out, in its bigger pot.

11th June 2024: It is **3.23 am** and I have still not been to sleep. I decided to switch the alarm clock off and see if that helps.

4.32 am, still awake. It is light enough to write this. I was getting the burning coming up a wee bit, so I decided to try sitting up and write this.

I know that Diane will understand if I was to be late and thought of putting the computer on to write an email to her and my boss, but I know that they will understand and that I don't need to do that.

Time to go to sleep. Let's see when I wake up.

I switched the alarm off at 3.30 and still hadn't fallen asleep by 4.30am but, amazingly, managed to wake up at the right time. Work went very well. I am tired but enjoyed getting back into my work.

14th June 2024: Well, that is me done my first week (I only work 3 days) back at work. I was very tired, but it all went great. I really enjoyed being back and soon got into the swing of it again.

As for the losing our jobs trouble. Well, we have to refight or, once again, tell them all about what we do. But the good news is, that now, even if we do lose them, it won't be until around this time next year. So, I have another year to get on with and won't have to think about it for now.

19th June 2024: I was back on the double decker bus today. I am back on the journey of life again. I went to Perth. I might not do that walk again, on my own, but it is lovely to know that I can. I saw an osprey with a fish although it was right across the river.

22nd June 2024:

(See Video Diaries on *See Salt Tears* Website 22nd June 2024)

25th June 2024: I am very tired and strangely, stressed, before the work meeting to tell me about getting another year to save our jobs. I have diarrhoea, a dry mouth, numb feet and bad eyes. I cried a bit in the meeting. I am so much better but anything that would have upset me a bit, usually, is now very multiplied. I wanted to leave work. But I have decided that if they think that they don't need me but will pay me for another year, then I should just make the most of it.

It is all so vague. I have given my evidence a load of times. They're acting as if it is a new thing. That makes me feel like nothing we have done makes the slightest difference, none of it is noticed, in any way. Diane is off but Janis sent me a nice email. That cheered me up. I love my job. I will just get on with it. I am so tired now. I am very surprised how set back I am today. I hope I will be good again by tomorrow. I will go and look out the window now, then I am off to bed early.

5th July 2024: I looked out of the "sunroom" window before going to sleep. There was an owl!! It was on the roof of the flats opposite. It flew down a bit and I just knew that it was an owl. It moved along the gutter, twice, to the edge of the building. Then went to sit on top of the telephone pole. I didn't want to get my camera in case I missed it, but I did. I didn't get a good photo as it was too dark. But it sat there for a bit, then flew straight towards me, up, over my head, and then, onto our roof. Magical. 😃🦉💚 I've just realised that a heart is also an owl's face.

(Synchronicity: I was typing, it was too dark" as the CD sang, "the same dark night" and then, "in the night" as I wrote, "night" there, in my notebook.)

16th July 2024: I looked out last night to see if I could see the owl. I could hear them. Eventually, I saw a shape on the chimney opposite, but I thought that it must be part of the plants. It turned out to be the owl, which flew away. I have seen it three times now. Yesterday, Dad used the word "owl" in our Facebook, Scrabble game.

I was told, in my head, that I would see an owl, clearly, and get a photo of it on Sunday. I didn't but I did see it on top of the telephone pole that night. It flew away as I went to get my camera though. An owl is one of my special signs, to watch out for me now.

I see faces a lot, in things now. I saw a Dr Who type monster face in a friend's funny horse photo. I saw a very happy, laughing face in the Amethyst Cathedrals' Facebook post of a Citrine crystal. It had a long, high alien head. They, the Amethyst Cathedral, said that it belonged to me now! I sometimes sketch the things, faces etc that I see in things, in my notebooks. I will put some of them in my *See Salt Tears* website Extras from Book page for you to see.

21st July 2024:

(See Video Diaries on *See Salt Tears* Website 21st July 2024)

22nd July 2024: I am very tired, yesterday and today. The owl was on the telephone pole tonight. It is getting darker, so harder to see but I know that it was it. A flock of crows flew over. After a while, the owl flew away. I saw its wings flutter and then it disappeared.

September 2024

1st September 2024:

(See Video Diaries on *See Salt Tears* Website 1st September 2024)

I got my telephone check-up last Monday. The lady was really nice. She listened to me. It was quite strange and sad to hear and talk about cancer again. It is much easier to just forget about it. She was saying that the radiotherapy can do a lot of things and that it keeps working away. Because it was only a week, I kind of didn't think it had done much. But since then, I have been sore under my boob along the hard rib line. She said to go back to putting the cream on and to carry on with the exercises. So, I have got another tube of my Calendula cream and will use that until it is finished. I think it needed done as that seems to have made things sore again. So, I think that they were needing moved. She was saying that it is good to do that now as, if the cancer was to come back, then it would be in a year or 2 and so it is good to get to know the new shape and feel of my boob now.

She also asked about a dry cough and burning coming up. I had forgotten that that could be from the radiotherapy too. I have been getting the burning but just a wee bit, at times, in the night and a dry throat. I thought it was allergies. I still get a very dry mouth in the evenings.

I got a bit fed up, after that, for the rest of the day, but had a good walk in the park, which is great for being in nature and having a good think about things. It is very therapeutic.

I am still very tired. I am trying to sleep in, a bit, on days that I am not doing things. I am sleeping well.

I am doing well. I have numb elbows and fingers, in the night. I have sore wrists today.

I put a new profile photo on Facebook today. It was a scary thing to do but it was time to do it. I didn't say anything. I reckon that my hair, really just looks, now, like I have a new hairdo.

I am working away on my new *See Salt Tears* website and really enjoying it. I get scared, at night, about it. I think of "baddies" controlling me, pinching my info etc. But I know it is good and the right thing for me to do.

8th September 2024:

(See Video Diaries on *See Salt Tears* Website 8th September 2024)

19th September 2024: My Advice: Anyone, no matter who, can get cancer. I have found that out for myself! I have known some lovely people who have died of cancer, some very close to me. I have also, known **many more**, who have got through it. Some who have had to have treatment and some who have not.

I would say that it is a very good idea to look after yourself mentally and physically. The current way our society deals with cancer, is to attack and destroy it. This is called treatment and it, mostly, keeps us alive but the fitter and healthier we are, I feel, the more we may be able to cope and deal with the treatment.

Personally, I don't think that it should be seen as a battle. Cancer is just a biological thing happening in our bodies and one day, I hope, society will find new ways of understanding what is going on. Why it is happening. Learning and working with it, rather than against it and finding ways to understand, listen and sort out just what it is trying to tell us. (Perhaps that might be a good answer to many other things in our society?!)

However, in the meantime, my advice to anyone facing such things would be **go and see the professionals**. They are wise and experienced. Put your trust in them. As soon as a lump is found. Either it is nothing to worry about, in which case that is great, you can put your mind at ease, or it is cancer in which case, the quicker it is sorted, the better. That was definitely the case, for me, as I had an aggressive, fast-growing type. So, go and get it checked if you are at all worried.

One thing everyone can be sure about, in life, is that one day we will die. We don't like to talk about that, but it is true. **Life is a journey, so make the most of it. Love and respect yourself, everyone and everything.** Whatever happens that is your own personal journey.

26th September 2024: My mouth is dry, and burning is coming up. I have been bruised on the back of my hand since Friday. I've been a bit worried about myself this week. I have been much more tired. Hopefully it is just a healing tired. I am still tired anyway, but this was different. I don't work on a Friday, so will have a long lie tomorrow.

Today, I had a massive panic. I got an email from my bank. They are, once again, changing, as they are being taken over by another company. The email was the usual sort of general email that we get from them. One bit of it said, in a red box, you will have to change your ISA over if you want to keep it tax free. I didn't really understand what it was saying, so thought that I better phone them to find out. I hate phoning things, generally. I hate phoning the bank as it is so vague, and I have no idea who or where I am phoning. I also hate when there is a big phone queue. But I thought that I would be good and give it a try.

I was stunned to get an answer very soon. The lady was lovely but couldn't help, so passed me on to someone else. I thought, oh no a queue this time, but no, there wasn't.

The lady was lovely, again. It took her a while to find out what I was going on about. Once she did, she said that the email sounded suspicious, like a con. I said that I didn't think that it was, as it was obviously from them and wasn't asking for any information or anything. She said that they are very good at these things and convincing. I was sure it was **not** a con. She got me to send her the email and said that she thought that it was a con but that it was all fine and my bank account was fine.

I went off the phone stunned. I couldn't believe it; it was such a convincing email, and I felt really silly. But I then had another massive panic as I thought that I had phoned the number on the email and, of course, I thought that it was the bank, so told them everything. They knew my phone number, email and details, address etc. I couldn't believe how stupid I'd been and how easy it was.

So, I went to my online banking page and phoned the number on there. Meanwhile it was past my work lunchtime, so my routines were all messed up too. But that was the least of my troubles!

I got another lovely lady. She kept me calm and helped me out. Trying to get me to explain what had happened. I was giving her my details when I stopped as, of course, I was having another panic. How did I know that she was not a con! She calmed me down and explained how I could check that the number, that I had phoned, was the right one.

Once she understood what I was on about, she said that she had received that same email too and that it sounded fine. We compared the emails, and it **was** from my bank, **not** a con!

It turned out that the other lady that I had talked to, did work for them and it was **all** fine!

My goodness, that was most definitely **not g**ood for my health. I let my workmate know it was all okay and took a long, late lunch break. I went the longer walk round and tried to get myself to breathe in the fresh air. That did me a load of good. In the supermarket, a lady was trying to get a meal deal, and it was not working. So, it took ages, but I stayed cheery and was joking with another lady in the queue. By the end of the walk, I had realised that life is good.

It is great to be cheery and I am very lucky to still be alive. I also worked out that, instead of it being a warning for me to **not** trust people, it was actually a sign for me to trust myself and to trust other people.

I have been worrying (in the night), a bit, about creating my *See Salt Tears* website, as anyone in the world could see it. But I have to just have trust and faith and this whole event, today, made me see and know that more.

I don't know what I will think about it tonight though. It certainly has not been good for my tiredness today and gave me back my fluttery heart.

I've got a bad headache now and my dry mouth, after writing that, but I think it was good for me to get it all written down.

Isn't it funny and ironic that the panic and worry of a con made me and another lady think that I had had a con, when I had not!

I said to the bank lady, who sorted it all out, that if they just gave us back our banks, in our towns, then these things would not happen. She agreed, saying, yes, then you could have just gone in and asked them.

27th September 2024: I woke up full of the cold.

29th September 2024:

(See Video Diaries on *See Salt Tears* Website 29th September 2024)

30th September 2024: I am seeing silver, electric lines when trying to open my eyes in the morning. I wonder if it is the visual migraine or connected with when they thought that I had that? Maybe I am more stressed than I think. I have a dry mouth too. I am worried and caring about my oldest brother, who is having a tough time at the moment. I am also worried about me, or rather getting the cancer back, subconsciously, I think.

Writing this down, I am thinking that I suppose it is like when I emerged after the Covid lock down. Emerging from this, and that, is when I had the visual migraine thing. I also have raised skin on my shoulder and round my collar bones.

My neighbour sent me an email today. She was woken up by the owls making a noise in the night and then thought that I was talking about them. She then quickly got back to sleep. I thought that this was a magical story to hear. I love owls and am so glad that it sounds like I am very connected to them.

October and November 2024

1st October 2024: Well, it's been quite a day, work wise! I found out about a load of extra work that we are getting to do. My work colleague told me, this morning, and it really stressed me out. I went my lunchtime walk, which really helped, but I just felt that I wanted to leave my work now, even although it would not be sensible, money wise. I love my work but this keeping getting told that we are losing our jobs is really not a good way to carry on. I am so tired again today. I think it is important to tell you about this as things stress me out and I get so tired even although I am doing so much better.

It is so frustrating when we are told that we are losing our jobs but then there is, also loads of work to do. It Is going to happen more and more in our society, where we ask for more and more money, to live on, as things are so expensive but there is not more and more money to give. I know money does not matter and is not what is important although we do need it to live on and do many things. We will all get on a lot better, I reckon, when we realise that material wealth is **not** what is important in life.

This afternoon, my boss told me about the extra work, and then we had a meeting. It was very stressful but also therapeutic, as we all said how we really felt about it all.

It is a strange mixture, as I am generally well and better, but it is important to let you know the truth of how I am doing. I try to be cheery and positive, and am, but I also want to let you know that it takes a long time to get through and over this journey.

6th November 2024: I was wondering what on earth the big pile of ailments in my notes were, but then I realised that they were notes so that I told the doctor everything when I ask about my left arm being numb in the night. So, this list is what I told her about:

My eyes have been tired with the silver lightning behind the lids and heavy again, for the last two nights. My left arm is sore and numb. I am uncomfy under my left rib and my ears had that numb thing, like they are folded in the night and the blood is cut off. My feet were numb in the bath, and I have my rash, hot flushes and an itchy head.

7th November 2024: I had my sore arm in the night. I didn't want to but wrote to the doctor.

I feel a bit silly now as I got an answer back that she will not be back until Monday but if there was anything else, then to let them know. So, it is obviously nothing to worry about.

I am pleased really, as I did not want to mess up Duncan's visit, our day out Friday or visit Saturday.

Hopefully it will all get better, and I will have forgotten about it by next week. It was right to ask about it though as it is the whole of my left arm.

12th November 2024: Well, I wish I had never sent the email to the doctor, last Thursday. This afternoon, while I was working, I got a phone call from the Health Centre with a message from the doctor that I had written to. I was advised that I was to make an urgent appointment with my opticians and that I have a doctor's appointment tomorrow afternoon.

My optician is in Perth. I knew, when they said I was to get an urgent appointment, that it would be like the last time and that I would have to go there pretty quickly. So, I phoned Dad first and he said he would take me through. Which was great as I then phoned the opticians and just got to Perth in time, to get my appointment.

She, the optician, said that my eyes are fine. Which is brilliant. She says that the trouble I am having, with not being able to open them in the night and seeing the silver lines, is maybe the visual migraines, or tired, or dry eyes. I reckon it might be all three. I do have my rash round my eyes which is dry. I am to use some cream to put in my eyes, before I go to sleep. That will help, if it is dry eyes. If it does not work, then it is not that and I am to just stop using it.

It is interesting because the man that was doing the eye tests for me, asked if I was retired, that is a couple of people recently that have assumed I was retired when asking my questions. That must be what happens when you have white curly hair!

Poor Dad had to drive home in the dark. But we did fine. My eyes are a bit blurry now, that happens from the drops that they put in for the tests. I think I will go to my bed early and hopefully sleep well for my work tomorrow.

13th November 2024: I got my doctor's appointment today and I am fine and hunky dory. The doctor was really nice and went through all my email.

I am to go to physio for my shoulder, it is a damaged tendon. I have got cream and wash stuff for my rash. I am to get a blood test for the tiredness, but it should be fine. It is a fasting blood test, so I am not to eat or drink anything but water from 10pm the night before, it is at 8.40 in the morning. That should be fine, it just means not having my breakfast.

So, all good.

I was reading the box of the cream, and it has steroids in it. I never want to be near another steroid in my life! Never mind I am sure it is a tiny amount and not like getting it pumped into my blood like the treatment did.

14th November 2024: Well, I was awake from 5am with my thumbs rubbing and my head not wanting to switch off. I was planning a Facebook page that would be used for staff, present and past, from work. It was all planned out! However, I managed to get up for work fine.

(I have thoughts, plans and ideas about all different sorts of projects, sometimes. Most of them never get past the idea or planning stage.)

My eyes were hard to open in the night and I saw the silver lines. The lines were shorter but also wider. But when I woke up, my eyes felt very much fresher. I have not felt so tired today.

My rash also seems to be getting better already. Brilliant and I am glad, now, that I did contact the doctor.

19th November 2024: The eye cream seems to be doing great. For about three nights, or more, I was still getting the silver lines, but my eyes are so much more refreshed in the morning. It still can be difficult to open my eyes in the night. It seems to have made me so much less tired. I wonder if some of the tired was just really tired eyes.

I had my physio appointment today for my sore shoulder. She got me from the waiting room and took me to her wee treatment room. She couldn't get my file to come up on the computer for a while, the computer must have been tired as it was late in the day! It worked in the end.

She then asked how she could help me. That stumped me a bit, as I thought it is you that is meant to tell me that, I have no idea! But I just told her about my sore shoulder, numbness in the night, etc. She listened, asked some questions and got me to stand up and try some arm movements etc.

I found it quite fascinating how much difficulty I had processing when both she and the doctor, the other day, asked me to do certain movements. Such as touching their hands and pushing them away from me. A couple of these instructions took me time to compute. I had to stop and think what they said first, then repeat what I thought they had said for the next bit, out loud, to check, such as "push away". I wonder if it was an autism processing thing with hearing a couple of the instructions at once and, also, having to tell my head and body what pushing their hand away was or whatever the instruction meant me to do. I find these occasional kinds of instances interesting as, of course, I know how to do what they are asking.

Anyway, the great news is that it is nothing bad. I have tendonitis. I am to carry on doing my exercises, that I was given and have been doing since my operation. I am also, throughout the day, to try and take notice and push my shoulders back and down.

That is it, so all fine and hunky dory.

21st November 2024: I was just thinking about my new hair and how I get a different reaction from people. I occasionally might see a man who catches my eye and think my usual, oh he won't be interested in me, but then it hits me, like waking up and remembering something bad has happened, that he is seeing an old lady now. But mostly, I love it. I get nicer, friendlier hellos and different reactions from people than I did before.

Anyway, thinking about all that, reminded me of a thing that happened to me in the supermarket a month or so ago. They have fitted doors all along the fruit, veg etc departments and it takes a bit of getting used to now, to open the doors. It kind of put me off my shopping for a while as my head couldn't get into "shopping mode" with the changes.

So, I was standing, trying to get my head to figure out how this particular new door opened to get out the veg that I wanted. When a lady stopped to say, "do you need a help with that?" I turned to look at her and started to say that it was okay, that I was just working out how the door opened, when she looked at me and said, "oh no sorry" and quickly backed away. She must have thought that I was a wee, old "wifie" with my curly white hair and then saw my face and realised that I wasn't. It was quite weird really but luckily I saw the funny side of it.

30th November 2024: My rash is quite bad or rather, not going away. It is on my left shoulder, a bit on both sides of my neck and round my eyes. A wee patch has appeared under my right chin. My eyes are still sometimes hard to open, and I can get the silver lines, like lightening, behind the right lid when I try to open it. My left side, under my ribs, feels uncomfortable when sitting in bed, reading and when sitting typing up my notes.

Maybe my rash got bad when I got the fright with Dad. We had a wee scare with him, after three scary days, we took him to the hospital. He was kept in overnight had all the possible tests you could think of, and he was told that he was perfectly fine. Which is brilliant. He seems fine now.

It is also stressful and very interesting typing up my notes for this book. I am still very tired. My eyes were bad today and my lip went all fizzy and twitchy.

Newton's Cradle

I was trying to think, in my bath last night, what I would call this last chapter of the book. I got a strong image of the "Newton's Cradle" executive desk toys that you used to get. Before the days of the internet and mobile phones, to keep us amused, people, especially, in those days, men, had desktop toys. The Newton's Cradle was a metal frame with silver-coloured balls hanging down from strings. I used to love those things, pulling back one or more of the balls and letting it go to hear the click, clack, of them all hitting each other and moving back and forward in their pattern.

They moved and worked together, made patterns, made noises, went on and on, then slowly but surely, settled down and joined back together again.

This journey has certainly shaken, cracked and thumped its way along but it has also flown in the same direction, leading towards where I am today.

It is time for me to stop writing this book now. Thank you very much for your company and I hope that you have enjoyed the journey through all its ups and downs.

The writing down of my thoughts and feelings, throughout this whole journey, has really helped. These notes, creating my website and writing this book, *See Salt Tears,* have all been a massive journey in themselves, quite apart from the actual journey that I have been through.

I have carried on for a while with my notes, partly because I wanted to show how long things take to heal, work out and work through. But also, because the creating and writing of them have, themselves, become a part of my life.

But that word, **life**, tells me something. I have started to get on and started, very slowly, to start living again. It is now time to stop writing this book. I hope that you have seen and understood the journey as experienced through these particular, autistic lens, "See" Salt Tears.

Bye for now and I look forward to meeting you again in my next book, whatever adventure that may take us on.

Let us hope that that is all for this kind of journey.

Find new ways. Stop the killing and find ways to listen to, understand and work with cancer and whatever else is causing us trouble or danger.

References

Books:

Brady, F. (2023) *Strong Female Character*. London: Hachette

Haddow, B. (2015) *Living Diagnosis*. CreateSpace Independent Publishing Platform

Haddow, B. (2020) *Answers Inside Out*. KDP

Jackson, L. (2002). Freaks, Geeks and Asperger Syndrome. London: Jessica Kingsley Publishers

Moorjani, A. (2012). *Dying to Be Me: My Journey from Cancer, to Near Death, to True Healing*. Carlsbad, CA: Hay House

Prince Harry. (2023). *Spare*. 1st ed. London: Bantam

Tolkien J. R. R. (14 Oct. 2021) *The Lord of the Rings*. HarperCollins; Single-volume illustrated edition

Wilcock, D. (2013). *The Synchronicity Key*. New York: Dutton

Games:

Cranium, Inc. (1998). *Cranium*. Board Game. Seattle: Cranium, Inc.

Kobbert, Max J. Dingbats. 2007. Board Game. Germany: Ravensburger Spieleverlag

Wizards of the Coast (2025) Magic: The Gathering Arena [online]

Past Times 2010, Bemused, Befuddled and Bewildered, Board Game, Past Times

Websites

My Facebook Photos Page: Bs Photos
https://www.facebook.com/BsPhotosWorld

Sea Salt Tears Website (my journey through cancer and life, coloured by an autistic lens):
https://seesalttears.wordpress.com/

Maggie's |Cancer help organisation:
https://www.maggies.org/

SWAN, For and by autistic women, girls and non-binary people:
https://swanscotland.org/

Wharmby, P., n.d. Pete Wharmby – Neurodiversity Speaker and Writer. Pete Wharmby. Available at:
https://petewharmby.com/

Other

Kübler-Ross, Elisabeth. 1969. *On Death and Dying*. New York: Scribner

Duracell, 1973. *Drumming Bunny*. [Television advertisement]

E.T. the Extra-Terrestrial (1982) Directed by S. Spielberg [Film]. Universal City, CA: Universal Pictures

Mrs. Palfrey at the Claremont (2005) Directed by D. Ireland [Film]. London: Metrodome Distribution

The Beatles. (1970) *'Let It Be'*, Let It Be

The Munsters (1964). Universal Television

Meet the Author

A cheery, friendly Scottish lady, Blanche loves whiling away the hours on long walks, capturing the beauty of nature through photography.

She has now written three books:

Living Diagnosis
Answers Inside Out
See Salt Tears

Art, reading, and computers are also big passions in Blanche's life.

Discover more about Blanche's world, including her photos, videos, and artwork, on her website:

See Salt Tears

Printed in Dunstable, United Kingdom